fabric art
collage
40+ MIXED MEDIA TECHNIQUES

Rebekah Meier

C&T PUBLISHING

Publisher: Amy Marson

Creative Director: Gailen Runge

Editors: Kesel Wilson, Terry Martin, and Cynthia Bix

Technical Editors: Sandy Peterson and Nanette Zeller

Copyeditor/Proofreader: Wordfirm Inc.

Cover/Book Designer: Christina D. Jarumay

Production Coordinator: Casey Dukes

Illustrator: Tim Manibusan

Photography by Christina Carty-Francis and Diane Pedersen of C&T Publishing, Inc., unless otherwise noted

Published by C&T Publishing, Inc., P.O. Box 1456, Lafayette, CA 94549

Library of Congress Cataloging-in-Publication Data

Meier, Rebekah,

  Fabric art collage : 40+ mixed media techniques / Rebekah Meier.

    p. cm.

  Summary: "Covering all of the basic supplies and techniques for creating mixed-media layered collage pieces, this book features 5 projects and a gallery of inspirational finished artworks"—Provided by publisher.

  ISBN 978-1-57120-580-3 (paper trade : alk. paper)

  1. Collage. 2. Textile crafts. I. Title.

  TT910.M445 2009

  702.81'2—dc22

                                    2008030567

Printed in China

10 9 8 7 6 5 4 3 2

ACKNOWLEDGMENTS

Thanks to Kesel Wilson, Sandy Peterson, Cynthia Bix, Christina Jarumay, and the entire C&T Publishing team for working with me to bring this book to fruition. Special thanks to my editor, Terry Martin, for keeping me calm and on track and being there when I needed you most! Additional thanks to all the manufacturers who supplied me with their wonderful products.

DEDICATION

I would like to dedicate this book to my family. To Brad, Dan, and Matt: I appreciate your patience, understanding, and willingness to help with the tasks of daily life. A special appreciation is reserved for my mom, who helps me daily with whatever I need done. I could not do what I do without you!

tents

introduction

Collage techniques date back to early Chinese history and the advent of paper. Collage pieces can also be found in the work of tenth-century Japanese calligraphers and in medieval European cathedrals of the thirteenth century. *Merriam-Webster's Dictionary* defines *collage* as "an artistic composition made of various materials (as paper, cloth, or wood) glued on a surface; a creative work that resembles such a composition in incorporating various materials or elements."

The term *mixed media* describes the techniques and materials used to create collage artwork. Mixed media combines paint, ink, fragments of paper and fabric, along with other art supplies and fusible adhesives, all layered together to create a work of art. These pieces can be flat, such as with quilts or canvas, or three-dimensional compositions, creating an assemblage. *Layers* are created as the parts or elements of the foundation or base work, whereas an *embellishment* is used to adorn and enhance the overall appearance of the finished artwork.

I use fabric in combination with mixed-media techniques to create unique collage art pieces. I hope that this book will inspire you to try the same. My interest in collage and mixed media was piqued when I first started reading magazines such as *Somerset Studio, Quilting Arts,* and

Cloth Paper Scissors. These publications made me eager to try new techniques and stretch my creativity. I have been creating collage and mixed-media artwork pieces for many years now. In my creative life, it is what I love doing the most.

As a designer working in the craft industry, my job is to come up with creative ideas and ways to use manufacturers' products. I also publish craft articles and projects using many different media. It seems only natural that I would be drawn to mixed media because I love working with different kinds of materials and techniques—from rubber stamps to fabrics. I also love to layer little snippets of techniques, combining them all to create my artwork. This book shows some of my favorite techniques, which I have discovered along my way. It also shows how I layer them to create my art. I hope the techniques in this book will inspire your creativity and artful adventures. For most techniques, I have listed generic names of products used. The brands I use follow in parentheses. Don't feel limited—feel free to experiment and try your own favorite brands.

tools and supplies

Most of the tools and supplies used in this book are available at your local craft and quilt stores or online. See Resources (pages 94–95) for contact information for product manufacturers and suppliers.

SAFETY TIPS

When using hot tools or when working with caustic chemicals, such as bleach, it is important that you take necessary safety precautions. Always wear safety glasses and a mask or respirator. Work in a well-ventilated area when using hot tools that come in contact with synthetic materials. Wear a mask when working with pigment and embossing powders, which can become airborne.

When using the Creative Textile Tool (see Sewing and Design Tools, page 12), protect your work surface by working on a tempered glass, heat-resistant mat or a ceramic tile.

FABRICS

Most of the fabrics used in this book are cotton quilting fabrics. I also like to use lightweight upholstery fabrics and unbleached muslin (a finely woven cotton cloth). Because I make art quilts that will never be washed, I do not prewash my fabrics. Other fun fabrics that I frequently use include the following:

Felt: Felt is a nonwoven material made by pressing fibers (usually wool) together into a unified cloth. I prefer working with wool/rayon felt, which is offered by National Nonwovens. The wool/rayon mix allows the felt to be hot stamped. Embossed felts are made from synthetic fibers. They can be bought off the bolt in the fabric department of most local craft stores.

Silk: Different types of silk fabrics are available. Lustrous 100% dupioni silk is often woven from two different colors of threads, so that it shimmers or changes color in the light. The silk woven yarn is uneven and varies in width, creating a series of natural horizontal "slubs," or a nubby texture. These should not be considered flaws; rather they add to the textile's character. This silk can be found in the bridal department of most fabric stores. Habotai is a soft, lightweight, lustrous silk made with a tight, plain weave and very fine yarns. Habotai, sometimes called China silk, has a limp, soft, thin sheerness and a slippery, smooth texture.

I usually purchase my silk from Dharma Trading Company. Another fun and easy option is Print on Silk inkjet fabric, manufactured by Jacquard. For the Silk Fusion technique (page 36), I use plain silk hankies purchased online or sold by YLI.

Quilt batting: Batting is traditionally used as the middle layer of a quilt sandwich. For my collages, I use batting in nontraditional ways; for example, as the base for needle felting (page 41) or for layering behind embellishments. I use Fairfield's Nature-fil Bamboo Batting. I love its silky feel and its sheen when it is dyed with tea or Rit dye.

Organza: Organza is a sheer, semitranslucent fabric that is great for layering. I buy it in ribbon form or off the bolt. I also use the inkjet-printable ExtravOrganza fabric by Jacquard.

Velvet: When embossing with a rubber stamp (see Embossed Velvet, page 56), I use velvet that contains rayon and acetate in the blend, so the velvet will not burn and will emboss properly. Any velvet ribbon is okay when using the Creative Textile Tool to doodle (see Etched Velvet, page 57). Experiment with other napped fabrics. Sometimes it is possible to use the Creative Textile Tool to doodle on upholstery fabrics that have a velvetlike appearance.

Tyvek: Tyvek is a strong, fabriclike material made from polyethylene fibers that is commonly used by shipping companies for their shipping envelopes and bags. You can recycle the Tyvek bags by using them as an embellishment or as the base for your mixed-media projects. Tyvek can be cut using stencils and the Creative Textile Tool (see Tyvek, page 66).

PAPER

Tissue and rice paper: Plain, ordinary gift tissue is a wonderful and inexpensive staple to have on hand. I like to paint it with Golden Fluid Acrylics or Ranger Adirondack Dimensional Pearls acrylic paints and use it as an embellishment or as a layer of the project. Rice paper has qualities similar to tissue and also makes a great layer when painted.

Watercolor paper: Painted and torn watercolor paper makes a great substrate on its own, or it can be placed behind embellishments for added interest. The weight of the watercolor paper you use depends on its purpose. If the paper will be a backing for a wallhanging, I use a heavier 140 lb sheet. If it will be used behind an embellishment, I use the lighter 90 lb weight.

Brown paper: Lunch or grocery brown paper bags can be painted and stamped with watercolors or acrylics to make a quick and easy custom-designed paper.

Parchment paper: Found in the grocery store and used for baking, parchment paper can also be used to protect projects from coming in direct contact with an iron.

Freezer and wax paper: Available at grocery stores, both of these papers are great for protecting your work surface. "Waste not, want not"—reuse these dripped-and dribbled-on papers by stamping, dry brushing, or dusting them with pigment powders. You can then use them as a layer behind any embellishment. In addition, C&T Publishing offers 8½″ × 11″ sheets of freezer paper (Quilter's Freezer Paper Sheets) that work great in inkjet printers.

Scrapbook papers: An endless supply of scrapbook papers is available in the marketplace. These papers can be painted with diluted acrylic paint or gesso, or stamped with pigment inks. Tear the painted papers and then reassemble and stitch them together for a paper patchwork (see Nontraditional Patchwork Fabric, page 38).

FUSIBLE AND STABILIZING INTERFACINGS

fast2fuse: This stiff, double-sided interfacing, available from C&T Publishing, comes in regular and heavyweight, and is sold in sheets or by the yard. It is fun to work with because it can be fused, even when painted (page 22); hot stamped with the Creative Textile Tool (see Hot Stamping, page 65); or cut into shapes and used as embellishments (page 65). I use both the regular weight and the heavyweight, depending on my project. For example, a book cover, Artist Trading Card (ATC), or postcard might require the stiffness of the heavyweight, whereas the regular weight is better for a project that needs a softer finished look and feel.

Steam-A-Seam 2: This iron-on fusible web, by The Warm Company, is sold in 9″ × 12″ sheets or by the yard. Release paper on both sides can be removed to expose the sticky surface. I use Steam-A-Seam 2 for making Tissue Fabric (page 33), Free-form Scrap Fabric (page 39), Altered Ribbon (page 47), and Nontraditional Patchwork Fabric (page 38). I also use it to finish the backing and binding of my art quilts.

806 Stitch-N-Tear: Made by Pellon, this product is traditionally used as a tearaway stabilizer or as interfacing for embroidery and appliqué projects. I like to use 806 Stitch-N-Tear because it has the qualities of both paper and fabric. I can cut it into 8½″ × 11″ sheets, paint it, or print on it from my home inkjet printer. Decorative shapes can also be punched from it using a paper punch or die-cutting machine (see Sizzix Machine in Sewing and Design Tools, page 13). This material can also be cut with the Creative Textile Tool (see Sewing and Design Tools, page 12) with or without a stencil.

Lutradur: This product, made by Pellon, is a 100% polyester, spun bond, nonwoven, translucent web. This strong, lightweight material can be painted, stitched, and cut with the Creative Textile Tool (see Sewing and Design Tools, page 12). Because of its strength and translucency, Lutradur makes a great layer in projects. It can be purchased online directly from Pellon.

Super Solvy: Available from Sulky, this water-soluble stabilizer is perfect for making Thread Fabric (page 44). It is strong enough that you don't need a hoop when doing free-motion embroidery stitching, and it washes away quickly and easily.

Solvron: Manufactured by Quilter's Resource, Inc., Solvron is a filament polyvinyl alcohol (PVA) fabric that dissolves easily in hot water. In this book, I describe using it as a texture element and as an embellishment (see Creating Texture, page 42).

Canvas: Panels and stretched canvas make a great base that can be built upon to create quiltlike artwork. It is easy to etch the surface of canvas using the Creative Textile Tool (see Sewing and Design Tools, page 12). I use Fredrix canvas panels, canvas pads, and stretched cotton canvas for my artwork. Look in the art department of your local craft store for these materials.

PAINTS, PIGMENT POWDERS, AND BRUSHES

Jacquard: I like to use Jacquard's Lumiere acrylic paint, Textile Colors (fabric paint), and Dye-Na-Flow products alone or mixed together. Lumiere paint is a metallic acrylic paint that I often use on embossed felt (page 20). I also mix Lumiere with Dye-Na-Flow and then paint it onto fast2fuse (page 23). Dye-Na-Flow is a thin, free-flowing liquid paint that is soaked up when applied to fast2fuse, giving great coverage. Jacquard's Colorless Extender can be blended with basic color paints to produce a lighter shade of that color.

Jacquard also makes Pearl Ex Pigment Powder. I love using these pigments whenever I need a pop of color or sparkle. Powdered pigments (also called pigmented mica powders) are dry, pigmented (colored) powders that have a metallic sparkle. They can be mixed into any medium or applied on their own to a surface such as paper or fabric. Powdered pigments are also great for highlighting hot-stamped designs on painted felt and fast2fuse (see Hot Stamping, page 65).

LuminArte: LuminArte products are easy-to-use, non-toxic, acid-free watercolors. The watercolors come in Radiant Rain Misters and Pure Color Concentrate Daubers (see Scotchgard, page 12). I also like to paint fast2fuse using LuminArte's Twinkling H2Os line (page 22), which come in watercolor cakes. LuminArte's Primary Elements Polished Pigments look beautiful when painted on wool felt (page 19) and silk (page 29), especially when mixed with their Simple Solutions #1. I especially like the delivery of the Radiant Rain Mister spray for quick color that can be applied directly onto any material. The color is very vibrant and concentrated. I love using the Primary Elements Polished Pigments to stamp onto silk (page 29). All of these products can be purchased online directly from LuminArte.

Golden: I like using Golden Fluid Acrylics for techniques such as painted Stitch-N-Tear (page 31) or for making Tissue Fabric (page 33). These acrylics are highly pigmented. Their thin consistency allows them to act almost like a dye. I mix these acrylics with water—a small amount goes a long way.

Ranger: I like to use Ranger's Adirondack Acrylic Paint Dabbers as paint applicators for foam and rubber stamps (page 26) and in techniques such as the Painting Felt with Bleach technique (page 21). I also like the Adirondack Dimensional Pearls acrylic paints because they dry very quickly and come in beautiful colors.

Shiva: Shiva Paintstiks are oil paints in solid, large-crayon form. Unlike traditional oil paint, Shiva Paintstiks usually dry within 24 hours. I like using them on muslin along with LuminArte Radiant Rain Misters (page 24). Shiva Paintstiks act like a resist when watercolor is applied to them, creating a nice effect.

Deval: Deval's fabric spray paint, Simply Spray, is nontoxic, nonflammable, permanent, and odor free. It does not need to be heat set, and it dries fast. I like to spray it onto embossed batting.

Krylon: I love using Krylon's Leafing Pens as a quick finish to edge around embellishments and fabric layers. They are available in gold, pale gold, copper, silver, and red shimmer.

Design Master: I use Design Master's Glossy Wood Tone spray paint to alter and distress fabrics and embellishments (see Spray Paint, page 72). When sprayed, it has a wonderful transparent appearance.

Varnish: DecoArt Liquid or Krylon Spray are made in three finishes—glossy, matte, or satin.

Brushes: Many of the techniques in this book require a paintbrush for applying paints, dyes, and medium. I use Loew-Cornell flat-shaped brushes, in widths up to $1^{1/2}$″, to apply matte medium, gel medium, Pearl Ex Pigment Powder, and ink. I use round-shaped brushes when painting with Twinkling H20 watercolors. I also use Loew-Cornell white bristle stencil brushes, ranging from $^{1/2}$″ to 1″ in size.

INKS AND DYES

Many kinds of inkpads and liquid inks are available. For the techniques in this book, I used the following types of inks.

Pigment inks: These inks are thick, opaque, and slow drying. I like to use Tsukineko Brilliance colors for stamping onto Stitch-N-Tear (page 31), Tissue Fabric (page 33), Easy Mixed-Media Patchwork Fabric (page 34), muslin (page 28) and silk (page 29). If the pigment ink does not dry quickly, Krylon's Workable Fixatif Spray (page 12) can be applied to set the pigment ink.

Watermark inks: These inks are used for embossing (page 63) and with pigment powders. When stamped onto a surface, watermark ink leaves a clear mark to which embossing and with pigment powders adhere. The project area is usually first stamped with a watermark-inked rubber or foam stamp. Next, embossing powder is applied, excess powder is shaken off, and heat is applied to raise the surface. Pigment powders—dry powder with metallic particles—can be applied directly on the stamp mark with a brush. I use VersaMark by Tsukineko.

Alcohol inks: These fast-drying inks are formulated to adhere to nonporous surfaces, but they also work beautifully on canvas. I use Ranger Adirondack Alcohol Inks for techniques such as etching onto canvas sheets (see Etched Canvas, page 62) and distressing buttons (see Paper Buttons, page 46).

Solvent ink: These permanent inks, such as StazOn from Tsukineko, are best for use on nonporous surfaces and when liquid, such as water, would smear the stamped design. I use StazOn when stamping tissue papers that will be used for the Tissue Fabric technique (page 33).

Dye inks: These fast-drying, water-soluble inks are sold in pad or liquid form (reinker) in a bottle. I like to use Ranger's Tim Holtz Distress Inks. For altering lace and trims, I use Ranger Adirondack Dye Reinkers mixed with water because it is in liquid form, which allows it to bleed when applied to the lace.

Rit Dye: I use Rit fabric dye to age, distress, and overdye my fabrics. To overdye fabric, apply paint or dye to an existing printed fabric to create a new tone or color from the original. Rit dye is widely available and found in most grocery stores. Be sure to follow the manufacturer's instructions. I especially like liquid Rit dye because it is premixed and ready to go when I need it.

EMBOSSING POWDERS

Embossing powders are resins that when melted with a heat tool, create a raised surface that adds dimension to both fabric and paper. I use Ultra Thick Embossing Powder (also called Ultra Thick Embossing Enamel, or UTEE) to finish edges of embellishments or edges of layers. This gives my projects a rougher, more granular finish. I also use regular embossing powder for such techniques as Embossed Batting (page 58), because regular embossing powder gives a smoother finish. Embossing powders are usually found in the rubber stamp section of craft stores or online.

ADHESIVES, STIFFENERS, MEDIUMS, AND PROTECTANTS

Beacon adhesives and stiffeners: Fabri-Tac adhesive (for fabric) and Zip Dry adhesive (for paper) are my choices for simple adhesion of paper and light embellishments. I use Stiffen Stuff spray fabric stiffener to add stiffness to my fabrics and for the Silk Fusion technique (page 36).

Bo-Nash Bonding Agent 007: This adhesive, which is sold in granule form, is set with an iron. Bo-Nash 007 is terrific to use whenever you need to bond two materials together. I especially like using this product with ExtravOrganza (see Fabrics, page 7) and with fabric layering techniques. Before ironing, always place a nonstick sheet or parchment paper over the materials you want to bond together.

J. T. Trading 404 Spray and Fix: This is a permanently repositionable adhesive that has no residue transfer. It is great for tacking layers together and holding stencils onto fabric, as shown with the Melted Crayon on Muslin technique (page 25). I also use J. T. Trading's Fabric Shield to protect the applied pigment powders.

DecoArt Fabric Painting Medium: This product is typically mixed with acrylic paint, making it suitable for fabric painting. For the Embossed Batting technique (page 58), the textile medium also acts like a stiffening agent to hold the embossed design.

Liquitex Matte Medium: I use Liquitex Matte Medium as the adhesive for such techniques as Easy Mixed-Media Patchwork Fabric (page 34). Typically, matte medium is mixed with acrylic paint and used to extend color and increase paint volume. It also is a great adhesive and is nonyellowing, flexible, and water resistant. I also use Liquitex Matte Gel Medium when adhering heavier embellishments, especially when working on canvas.

Krylon Workable Fixatif: I use Krylon's fixative spray as a reworkable clear finish that prevents smudging or lifting of art materials. Once the Fixatif is sprayed on the surface, another medium can be applied on top.

Ranger: Ranger's Inkssentials Glossy Accents, a clear gloss medium, makes a great protective coating when creating Paper Beads (page 50).

Scotchgard: After using Radiant Rain Misters with techniques such as Shiva Paintstiks on Muslin, Silk Fusion, Etched Velvet, organza ribbon (Needle Felting), and Thread Fabric, spray a protective coat of Scotchgard onto the finished design.

THREADS AND FIBERS

YLI Corporation: I use fibers and yarns from YLI Corporation. I like using their thread, Multi's Embellishment Yarn, Painters Potpourri packs filled with fibers, Painters Mailing and Trading Cards by Tentakulum Manufaktur, silk hankies, and silk carrier rod waste. I also use YLI's metallic and quilting threads.

Gutermann: I use Gutermann threads for machine stitching and for "stitch doodling" free-motion embroidery designs onto fabric (page 43).

Angelina and Crystalina fibers: Angelina and Crystalina fibers, by Meadowbrook Inventions, are made from polyester filaments and most bond together when heat is applied. Fusing occurs when the fibers are placed between two sheets of parchment paper and quickly ironed. The result is a wispy, thin sheet of shimmering color that can be used as a layer. I also like to cut fused Angelina fibers into small shapes for use as embellishments. Fused Angelina can also be embossed with a rubber stamp for a more artful embellishment.

SEWING AND DESIGN TOOLS

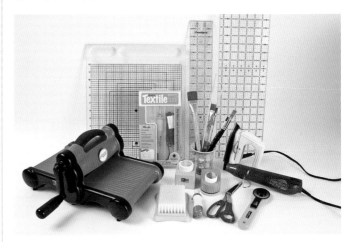

3-in-1 Color Tool: This tool, offered by C&T Publishing, is based on the Ives color wheel. It helps you choose or match colors with complete accuracy.

Sewing machine: You will need a sewing machine in good working order. Before beginning a new sewing project, take a moment to clean your machine of lint and stray threads. My sewing machine has a number of different decorative stitches, an attached even-feed foot, and, best of all, an automatic thread cutter. Although decorative stitches are fun to use, you can make some wonderful designs with a simple straight-stitch machine. Use your imagination!

Needle-felting tools: Needle-felting embellishing machines use barbed needles to create a piercing action that embeds fibers (or fabrics such as organza) into a base fabric (such as felt). There are several types of machines; try using them at your local dealer's to see which one fits your needs and budget. A less-expensive alternative is to use the handheld Clover Felting Needle Tool with brush pad, or individual felting needles.

Creative Textile Tool: Walnut Hollow's Creative Textile Tool is a hot tool that looks similar to a wood-burning pen. Its temperature makes it very useful for fabric. The Creative Textile Tool comes with seven points that are perfect for hot stamping, fusing, and cutting synthetic fabrics. It is found in craft and hobby stores or online directly from Walnut Hollow. There are also many other decorative points that can be purchased separately as attachments. When working with the Creative Textile Tool, I protect my work surface with a heat-resistant, tempered glass mat.

Iron: For techniques such as Melted Crayon on Muslin (page 25), I use a small travel iron.

Heat (embossing) gun: Heat guns, which are used for the Embossed Batting technique (page 58), are found in the rubber stamp section of craft stores.

Rotary cutter, rulers, and self-healing cutting mats: These are a quilter's must-have items! I use Omnigrip products for cutting and measuring. I like their nonslip rulers and rotary cutters, which help provide great precision and accuracy when cutting. I love—and cannot do without—their Dritz Quilting disappearing fabric markers.

Sizzix Machine: I use this die-cutting machine to cut simple shapes like circles and squares to enhance mixed-media techniques such as painting felt (page 20). Sizzix offers many designs, and their products are available online or in crafts stores.

Sizzix die-cutting machine

CREATIVE ACCESSORIES

Quilter's Vinyl: This great product from C&T Publishing is perfect for making Paper Buttons (page 46).

Rubber stamps: Deep-etched stamps work best for the embossing and stamping techniques in this book. I clean my rubber stamps with baby wipes.

Foam stamps: I use Making Memories foam stamps, as well as the ones found at the craft store in the paint department. Foam stamps are easily cleaned with soap and water.

Craft foam: This synthetic foam material is sold in sheets and found in the craft and children's section of most craft stores.

Clip art: The Vintage Workshop has many vintage clip art images and patterns that can be downloaded and printed from an inkjet printer. It is also a good source for inkjet fabric and canvas.

Crayons: I used Crayola Metallic FX Crayons for the Melted Crayon on Muslin technique (page 25). These crayons are hard to find in stores but can be ordered online at www.dickblick.com.

Fabric markers: I love and can't do without the Dritz Quilting disappearing fabric markers.

Grip-n-Grip: This nonslip sheet from Bear Thread Designs goes under your project to keep your fabric or stencil from moving or shifting when you are using Shiva Paintstiks (see Paints, Pigment Powders, and Brushes, page 10).

Brass stencils: I use Dreamweaver's or Plaid's brass stencils with the Creative Textile Tool when cutting embellishments using Lutradur and Dryer Sheets (page 68), or Tyvek (page 66).

Plastic stencils: Many inexpensive plastic stencils are available at craft stores. These stencils are usually found near the acrylic paint section.

Foil: Foil can be applied in several ways by using a foil adhesive or a fusible web. My favorite method is to apply the foil using a fusible web such as Steam-A-Seam 2. I order my foil from Laura Murray's website (see Resources, page 94).

Metal findings: To embellish my artwork, I often use metal findings, such as charms, fasteners, pendants, and filigree components traditionally used for jewelry making. The two companies that I most often use are Nunn Design and Vintaj.

Dowel rods: Dowel rods in varying sizes and materials can be found in most craft and hardware stores.

Buttons make great embellishments on a needle-felted pillow cover with stitch doodling details.

Save leftover technique scraps—even the smallest scrap can be turned into a lovely pin or embellishment.

Metal rulers and decorative-edge scissors: Metal rulers (with straight or decorative edges) and decorative-edge scissors can be found in the art and scrapbook departments of most craft stores.

Embroidery floss: DMC embroidery floss comes in six-strand bundles and can be found in the stitchery section of craft stores. The floss can be separated into strands and used accordingly.

Blue painter's tape: Rolls of this tape can be found in the paint section of a craft or hardware store. This tape is great because it sticks to the project surface but will not lift off paint when removed.

Paper punches: Many brands and styles of paper punches can be found in the scrapbook section of craft stores.

Cheesecloth and cosmetic sponges: These items can be found at both craft and grocery stores.

Scissors: To ensure longevity and sharpness, dedicate one pair of scissors for fabric and one pair for paper. Buy the best pair of scissors that your budget will allow.

Needles: Embroidery needles can be found in the stitchery section of craft stores. I buy them in packs and use the size appropriate for the embroidery stitches to hold the buttons and embellishments I'm adding to a project.

Craft trays: Place these shallow, open plastic containers under the surface to which you are applying embossing powders or glitter. The unused powders can then be returned to the jar using the hole on the side of the craft tray. Craft trays can be purchased in any craft store and are usually found near the glitter and embossing powders.

Palette paper: Use this palette, made by Loew-Cornell, when separating and blending your paint colors.

Beads, buttons, and brads: I like using old buttons that I find at garage sales and flea markets. Craft and fabric stores can also be a great source for new buttons. Beads can be found in the jewelry-making section of craft stores. In addition, independent bead stores offer a vast and beautiful selection of beads and baubles for adorning fabric and quilts.

Project scraps can be incorporated into any piece.

painting
and stamping

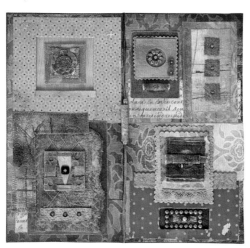

Various techniques with stenciled and stamped designs

Paint can be incorporated into fabric art in endless ways. Whether it is stenciled, dry brushed, stamped, or applied with another favorite method, paint can add a unique quality to your finished project. It can also be used to change the color of a fabric or to add color to plain synthetic materials such as fast2fuse.

Painted and stamped media are a great starting point for any project. Use the following techniques to add visual interest to an existing work or to create interesting pieces that can be incorporated into a base material (see Creating Base Material, page 31). Remember to follow the manufacturer's instructions to set the paint, if necessary.

STENCILING WITH PAINT

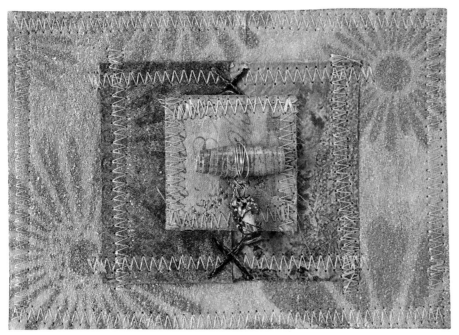

Postcard with stenciled fast2fuse

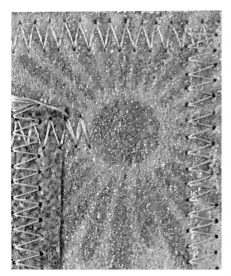

Detail of stenciled paint on fast2fuse

Great results can be achieved when stenciling paint onto fabric. It is perfectly (and uniquely) acceptable to have shadows and highlights when the stencil is removed to reveal the design.

MATERIALS

▧ Fabric

▧ Acrylic paint

▧ Blue painter's tape or repositionable spray adhesive

▧ Stencil brush

▧ Paper plate or palette paper

▧ Paper towels

HOW TO

1. Use tape or repositionable spray adhesive to secure the stencil to the fabric. This will keep the stencil from shifting.

2. Place a small amount of paint onto a paper plate or palette paper.

3. Barely dip the flat head of the stencil brush into the paint, then tap the loaded brush on a paper towel to remove the excess. You do not want your brush overly loaded with paint.

4. Gently tap the loaded paintbrush onto the fabric with a straight up-and-down or gentle swirling motion. Lift the stencil to reveal the stenciled image.

Tap paintbrush onto stencil.

Lift stencil to reveal image.

DRY BRUSHING WITH PAINT

Artist Trading Card with dry-brushed paint on muslin

Detail of dry-brushed paint

Dry brushing creates a great starting layer for a mixed-media piece and is an effective way to distress surfaces such as fabric or paper. The results of dry brushing look best when uneven and when some of the surface shows through the paint.

MATERIALS

▪ Fabric or any desired surface

▪ Acrylic paint

▪ Flat paintbrush

▪ Paper plate or palette paper

▪ Paper towels

▪ Blue painter's tape

HOW TO

1. Use blue painter's tape to anchor the fabric to a hard surface before painting.

2. Dip the tip of a flat paintbrush into paint.

Load brush with paint.

3. Remove the excess paint by brushing the brush head back and forth on paper towels. The paint on the brush should be almost dry.

Remove excess paint onto paper towel.

4. Use the almost-dry brush to apply paint to the fabric or other desired surface. Brush in a back-and-forth motion until the desired amount of paint is applied. The result should be an uneven appearance. **Note:** This technique also works well with ink, or try using watercolors for a soft effect.

PAINTING WOOL FELT WITH POLISHED PIGMENTS

Artist Trading Card with pigment-painted, hot-stamped felt

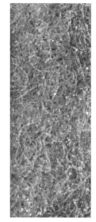

Detail of pigment paint on Artist Trading Card

Wool felt has long been a favorite medium of mine. When I first started experimenting with mixed-media techniques, wool felt was a natural material to begin with, because it is reasonably priced, readily available, and nonwoven so it doesn't unravel— a wonderful mix of attributes.

I absolutely love the beautiful shimmer that polished pigments create when they are mixed and applied to wool felt. The pigments are very vibrant and blend well into each other. Once created, the painted felt can be stamped with hot, rubber, and foam stamps (see the stamping techniques on pages 65, and 26–27), die-cut into shapes, and used as a substrate for art quilts or embellishments. The possibilities are endless!

MATERIALS

- Wool felt
- Polished pigment powders, 3 colors (LuminArte Primary Elements Polished Pigments)
- Simple Solutions #1 for fabric (LuminArte)
- Spray bottle filled with water
- Paintbrushes, 1 flat brush per color
- Paint tray or mixing container such as a recycled margarine container or laundry detergent cap
- Freezer or wax paper
- Latex gloves (optional)

HOW TO

1. Place the wool felt on freezer or wax paper to protect the underlying surface. Spray the felt with water until it is saturated and moist.

2. Pour a small amount of Simple Solutions #1 onto the paint tray. Dip the paintbrush first into the Simple Solutions #1 and then into the polished pigment powder. Work the brush back and forth to load the brush with pigment.

3. Paint the felt with the loaded paintbrush. You can also wear Latex gloves and work the pigment into the felt by hand as shown on page 22.

4. Repeat Steps 1–3 with other pigment colors. Use a separate paintbrush for each color.

5. Set the felt aside to dry.

6. When the felt is dry, paint dots, swirls, or stencil designs onto the felt with the polished pigment powder/Simple Solutions #1 mix for added effects. For even more unexpected results, spray the felt with bleach (see Painting Felt with Bleach, page 21).

Add additional details.

 TIP

These pigments are *highly* concentrated, so use only a *small* amount. For a more pastel effect, use more water to saturate the felt and/or more Simple Solutions #1 on the brush.

PAINTING EMBOSSED FELT

Postcard with painted, embossed felt

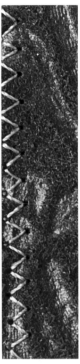

Detail of painted, embossed felt

Synthetic embossed felt is wonderful to work with. Once it is painted with a metallic acrylic paint, the recessed portions are more prominent, giving it a more textural appearance. I like to die-cut the painted, embossed felt into shapes or use it as a layer behind embellishments.

MATERIALS

- Embossed felt
- Metallic acrylic paint (Lumiere by Jacquard)
- Pigmented mica powder (Pearl Ex Pigment Powder by Jacquard)
- Fabric protector (Fabric Shield by J. T. Trading; optional)
- Flat paintbrush
- Freezer or wax paper

HOW TO

1. Place the embossed felt on freezer or wax paper to protect the underlying surface.

2. Shake or stir the acrylic paint.

3. Load the paintbrush liberally with acrylic paint. Paint the embossed felt in a back-and-forth motion. Completely cover the felt with acrylic paint, dabbing it into the crevices of the felt.

 TIP

When the felt is dry, you can use a paintbrush or your finger to apply additional highlights with the pigmented mica powder. If you wish, protect the pigmented mica powder from coming off the felt by spraying with Fabric Shield, a fabric protector from J. T. Trading used to protect against spills, dust, and dirt.

PAINTING FELT WITH BLEACH

Detail of bleached felt

Postcard with painted and bleached felt and hand-embroidery stitches

I like this technique because the results are always unpredictable. The bleach removes some of the color from the wool felt, leaving a mottled appearance. Adding layers of stamped images and outlining them with leafing pens adds interest and the satisfaction of creating your own custom-designed fabric.

MATERIALS

- Wool felt
- Acrylic dabber paint, 2–3 colors (Ranger Adirondack Acrylic Paint Dabbers)
- Small spray bottle filled with 100% bleach
- Leafing pen (Krylon)
- Foam stamps
- Freezer paper
- Stencil (optional)

HOW TO

1. Place the felt onto freezer paper and spray it randomly with full-strength bleach. Let the felt dry completely. The felt should have a mottled appearance.

2. Apply the acrylic dabber paint to the foam stamp.

Apply acrylic paint to stamp.

3. Stamp the image onto the bleached felt. If desired, repeat with another painted foam stamp.

Stamp image onto felt.

4. Outline the stamped images randomly with the leafing pen. If the pen snags on the felt, use a tapping motion around the image or use the side chisel of the pen.

Outline image with leafing pen.

VARIATION

Spray bleach through a stencil onto the wool felt. The bleached felt can then be stamped, stenciled, or left as is.

Spray bleach through stencil.

PAINTING FAST2FUSE WITH WATERCOLORS

Artist Trading Card with watercolor-painted fast2fuse and stitch-doodling embellishment

Detail of watercolor-painted fast2fuse

I love finding new uses for tried-and-true products like fast2fuse. One of my favorite ways to use it in my collage projects is to paint it. Even when painted, it still retains its fusibility, allowing fibers and fabrics to be fused onto it. It can also be rubber stamped, hot stamped, or die-cut into shapes, such as frames. Free-motion embroidery can also be applied to it. Little projects, such as tags, Artist Trading Cards (ATCs), and postcards, are also perfect for fast2fuse.

MATERIALS

- fast2fuse (C&T Publishing)
- Watercolor paints, several colors (Twinkling H20s by LuminArte)
- Spray bottle filled with water
- Matte medium
- 1 round watercolor paintbrush per color
- Freezer paper
- Latex gloves (optional)

HOW TO

1. Place the fast2fuse on freezer paper to protect underlying surfaces. Spray the fast2fuse with water.

2. Wet the tops of the watercolor pots by spraying them with water.

3. Paint the fast2fuse with several colors of watercolor paints. The colors will magically bleed and flow into each other, creating a kaleidoscope of color. Additional water can be misted onto the fast2fuse to further blend and mute the colors and speed up the coverage.

Paint watercolor onto fast2fuse.

4. If desired, manually work the colors into the fast2fuse. With gloved hands, scrunch and wad the fast2fuse, moving the color all the way through and to each edge.

Work colors into fast2fuse.

5. After the fast2fuse is dry, apply 2 coats of matte medium. Let the first coat dry before applying the next. This seals the fast2fuse and prevents the color from lifting.

PAINTING FAST2FUSE WITH DYE-NA-FLOW

Quilt with stenciled fast2fuse, hot stamped felt, and fast2fuse embellishments

Detail of stenciled fast2fuse

Fast2fuse retains its shiny appearance and fusibility, even after being painted. Fast2fuse painted with Dye-Na-Flow is great to use as an embellishment, as a background for quilts, and for book covers.

MATERIALS

- fast2fuse (C&T Publishing)

- Dye-Na-Flow (Jacquard)

- Metallic acrylic paint (Lumiere by Jacquard; optional)

- Spray bottle filled with water

- Plastic stencil

- Stencil brush

- Flat paintbrush

- Freezer paper

HOW TO

1. Place the fast2fuse on freezer paper and spray it with water so that it is damp.

2. Using a back-and-forth motion with the flat paintbrush, completely cover the fast2fuse with the Dye-Na-Flow paint. A small amount of metallic acrylic paint can be mixed into the Dye-Na-Flow paint for added sparkle.

3. Once the fast2fuse is dry, stencil a design onto it with acrylic paint (see Stenciling with Paint, page 17).

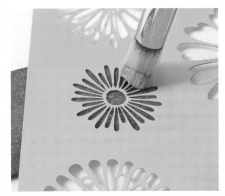

Stencil Dye-Na-Flow-painted fast2fuse with acrylic paint.

SHIVA PAINTSTIKS ON MUSLIN

Board book with oil paintstick designs

Detail of oil paintstick design

Shiva Paintstiks are oil paint in crayon form. The skin covering the top of the crayon can be removed by rubbing with a paper towel or by peeling with a knife. These paints can be applied to fabric by rubbing the paintstick over a textured sheet to reveal a design or by drawing directly onto the surface. **Note:** The paint can also be applied to paper with a stencil brush. To do so, load the stencil brush with paint by brushing it across the top point of the paintstick. Another way to use paintsticks with stencils is to color directly onto the palette paper, then swirl the stencil brush into the color and apply paint to the surface in a circular motion.

MATERIALS

▨ Unbleached muslin

▨ Oil paintsticks (Shiva Paintstiks)

▨ Watercolor spray paints, 2 colors (LuminArte Radiant Rain Misters; optional)

▨ Repositionable craft spray adhesive

▨ Deep-etched foam or rubber stamps

▨ Rubber craft sheet (Grip-n-Grip)

▨ Freezer paper

HOW TO

1. Place the deep-etched foam stamp with its image side up on the rubber craft sheet.

2. Spray the muslin with repositionable craft spray and place it adhesive side down onto the foam stamp.

3. Following the manufacturer's instructions, peel the protective film from the top of the paintstick.

4. Rub with the paintstick to transfer the image onto the muslin.

Rub paintstick across foam stamp.

5. After the paint has dried (approximately 24 hours), place the muslin onto freezer paper. You may spray a light amount of watercolor paint onto the muslin for added effect.

VARIATIONS

✻ To add more interest, repeat this technique and apply another stamped layer of color over the existing images.

✻ This technique also works well with silk instead of muslin.

MELTED CRAYON ON MUSLIN

Board book with melted crayon on muslin and felt bead

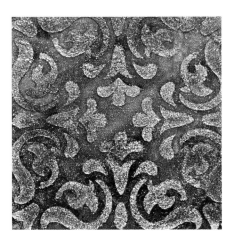

Detail of crayon on muslin

I like the results of this very versatile technique, because you end up with two design options. The first is the stenciled raised image, and the second is the flat design created by cleaning the stencil onto the muslin.

MATERIALS

- Tea-dyed muslin (see Distressing with Tea or Coffee, page 71)
- Crayons, metallic and regular (Crayola Metallic FX)
- Varnish, liquid or spray (DecoArt Liquid or Krylon Spray in desired finish—glossy, matte, or satin)
- Repositionable craft spray adhesive (J. T. Trading 404 Repositionable Craft Spray and Fix)
- Brass stencil
- Flat paintbrush (if using liquid varnish)
- Small travel-sized iron*
- Fine sandpaper
- Paper towels
- Tempered glass, heat-resistant mat (Walnut Hollow)
- Solvent cleaner
- Freezer paper

*Note: Travel irons do not have holes on the bottom to clog.

HOW TO

1. Place the muslin on a glass mat with freezer paper on top to protect underlying surfaces. Set the travel iron to the highest setting.

2. Melt several colors of crayon onto the muslin by holding the crayons directly against the hot surface of the travel iron and letting the drips fall to the fabric.

Melt crayons onto muslin.

3. In a back-and-forth motion, move the colors around with the iron, covering the entire piece of muslin until it is a smooth surface. Let the fabric cool.

Crayon-covered muslin

4. Clean the iron by dragging it across the paper towel and removing the excess crayon.

5. Spray the back of the brass stencil with repositionable spray craft adhesive. Place the brass stencil, sticky side down, onto the crayon-covered muslin. To ensure success, make sure that the stencil is completely secured to the muslin so that the crayon will not seep under the stencil.

6. Melt 2 to 3 colors of metallic crayon colors onto the stencil. Iron over the brass stencil, moving the crayon across the stencil.

Melt 2–3 metallic crayons onto stencil.

Use wiping motion to press brass stencil with iron.

7. Let cool and then remove the stencil to reveal the image.

Raised image revealed

8. Place the cooled stencil onto a new piece of muslin and iron over it. This will remove the excess crayon and will also color a new piece of muslin. Repeat several times. Completely clean the stencil by gently sanding it with fine sandpaper or by using a solvent cleaner.

9. Paint or spray a protective coat of varnish onto the raised crayon image.

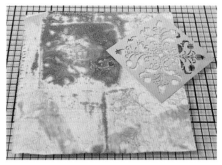

Move stencil around muslin, removing crayon from stencil.

STAMPING WITH FOAM STAMPS

Postcard with layers of painted, foam-stamped designs, tissue fabric, and paper button

Foam stamps are inexpensive and versatile. I like the flexibility they provide, especially where a little extra "give" is needed when stamping onto an uneven surface. Due to their easy cleanup and durability, foam stamps are also a great choice when using paint.

MATERIALS

■ Muslin or paper

■ Foam stamp

■ Watercolor, acrylic, or metallic acrylic paint (such as LuminArte's Twinkling H20s, Golden Fluid Acrylics, or Jacquard's Lumiere)

■ Flat paintbrush

Detail of postcard

HOW TO

1. Place a small amount of paint on the shiny side of freezer or scrap paper or dip the tip of the paintbrush directly into the paint.

2. Load the flat paintbrush with paint. Apply paint to the foam stamp. The stamp should have a thin, even layer of paint. With watercolors, using less water will result in a clearer image.

Load stamp with paint.

3. With the painted stamp facing down, press it onto the fabric or paper.

Stamp image onto muslin.

STAMPING WITH RUBBER STAMPS

Postcard with ink rubber-stamped muslin and tissue fabric embellishment

Detail of postcard with ink rubber-stamped muslin

Rubber stamps are a basic staple to have on hand when creating mixed-media techniques. They are readily available and come in many designs and themes that can be used for background designs or to create textural effects such as embossing velvet (page 56).

MATERIALS

- Paper or fabric
- Inkpad
- Rubber stamp

HOW TO

1. Lay the stamp on a flat surface with the image side facing up.

2. Load the stamp by lightly patting the inkpad onto the stamp.

3. With the inked stamp facing down, press it onto the fabric or paper.

Press inked stamp onto fabric.

 TIP

I often use a cosmetic sponge to apply ink to paper or fabric. Doing so gives the fabric or paper a vintage pop of color. Simply dab the cosmetic sponge onto the inkpad and lightly pat the sponge onto fabric or paper.

LAYERED PAINTING AND STAMPING ON MUSLIN

Artist Trading Card with dry-brushed muslin and hot-stamped felt embellishment

Detail of dry-brushed paint and layered stamping on muslin

I love the idea of designing my own fabric. Layering stamped designs onto fabric allows you to choose the color and design that is perfect for use in your artwork. Inexpensive muslin is a great staple to have on hand. I like to use it as a painted base for this stamping technique.

MATERIALS

- Muslin (I prefer to use tea-dyed muslin; see Distressing with Tea or Coffee, page 71)
- White textile acrylic paint (Textile Color by Jacquard)
- Colorless Extender (by Jacquard)
- Metallic acrylic paint, assorted colors (Lumiere by Jacquard)
- Spray bottle filled with water
- Assorted foam stamps
- Flat paintbrushes
- Freezer paper

HOW TO

1. Place the muslin on freezer paper to protect underlying surfaces. Mist the muslin lightly with water.

2. Dry brush white textile acrylic paint (See Dry Brushing with Paint, page 18) onto the muslin. Apply more paint in some areas than others to create an uneven appearance.

3. Use a flat paintbrush to apply a coat of Colorless Extender onto the painted muslin. This will mute the colors and allow more time for them to blend together.

4. Before the first coat dries, apply a new color of metallic acrylic paint to the muslin. Blend the colors in a back-and-forth motion, creating a soft, consistent, variegated appearance.

5. Repeat dry brushing and blending with another color. Add as many colors as desired.

Apply another color of metallic paint.

6. When the muslin is dry, apply metallic acrylic paint to the foam stamp with a paintbrush and stamp it onto the painted muslin.

7. Repeat Step 6 with other stamps, layering and overlapping the designs. I usually start with geometric shapes, such as diamonds, circles, and squares. The first stamped layers can be faint. Subsequent layers can be increasingly darker, building up the depth of the design.

Stamp design onto muslin.

LAYERED PAINTING AND STAMPING ON SILK

Artist Trading Card with polished pigment–stamped silk

Layered stamping also works well when applied to silk. Silk has a luxurious quality that, when painted, adds a delicate character to collage projects. When working with silk, use polished pigments with Simple Solutions #1 instead of acrylics. With polished pigments, using less liquid will produce more sparkle and darker color.

MATERIALS

- Silk fabric
- Polished pigments (Primary Elements Polished Pigments by LuminArte)
- Simple Solutions # 1 for fabric (LuminArte)
- Spray bottle filled with water
- Assorted foam stamps
- Round paintbrush
- Freezer paper
- Latex gloves (optional)

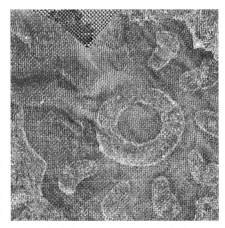

Detail of polished pigment–stamped silk on Artist Trading Card

HOW TO

1. Follow the same general instructions for applying and layering colors as you did with Painting Wool Felt with Polished Pigments, page 19. For best results, apply light colors first and then graduate to darker shades. The colors will run and bleed into each other, creating a beautiful effect.

2. Stamp the images lightest to darkest as well.

3. For added texture, scrunch and wad the silk with your hands as if you were removing liquid from a sponge, forming the silk into a ball after applying each color. When finished scrunching, lay the silk flat, keeping the texture effect intact.

4. When finished applying colors, use your hands to flatten out the silk and let it dry on freezer paper.

creating
base material

Quilt with base of free-form scrap fabric

The base material techniques in this section provide the foundation or starting point from which you can layer artwork to create dazzling effects. The techniques will provide unique foundations for quilts, Artist Trading Cards, and postcards. These foundations can also be punched, die-cut, or freely cut into shapes and used as an embellishment layer. Many of these techniques make frugal use of project scraps, such as fabric, tissue, and fibers.

LUTRADUR AND LACE

Artist Trading Card with Lutradur and lace base

Lutradur (see Tools and Supplies, page 9) is a very unique and versatile product. I love that it is semitranslucent while still retaining its strength, even when distressed. This technique is a great way to use up scraps of lace and trims left over from other projects. Use the finished piece as an embellishment or as a great background for a collage.

MATERIALS
- Lutradur
- Lace and trims
- Metallic acrylic paints, 2–3 colors (Lumiere Metallic, including Hi-Lite color by Jacquard)
- Matte medium
- Flat paintbrush
- Freezer paper

HOW TO

1. Place the Lutradur on the freezer paper to protect the underlying surfaces. Paint the Lutradur with a thin layer of matte medium to act as the adhesive.

2. Lay strips of lace and trims on the Lutradur in a random manner. Apply more matte medium, covering the lace so that it adheres to the Lutradur. Let dry completely.

3. Paint the lace with several colors of acrylic paint. Let it dry.

4. Dry brush highlights of acrylic paint onto the Lutradur and lace in a random manner (see Dry Brushing with Paint, page 18).

Decorate Lutradur with acrylic-painted lace.

STITCH-N-TEAR

Postcard with painted Stitch-N-Tear base and inkjet-printed designs

Stitch-N-Tear has qualities of both fabric and paper, which makes it great for mixed-media projects. When adorned with paints and images, Stitch-N-Tear makes great book pages and covers. It has the flexibility of fabric but can be torn like paper. Tearing with a decorative-edge metal ruler yields a textural edge that can be quite enjoyable!

MATERIALS

- Tearaway stabilizer (806 Stitch-N-Tear)
- Acrylic paints, 2–3 colors (Golden Fluid Acrylics)
- Pigment inkpads, 2–3 colors
- Workable fixative (Krylon Workable Fixatif)
- Liquid varnish
- An image of your choice (I used an image from The Vintage Workshop.)
- Rubber stamps
- Paper punches
- Metal rulers (with decorative edges)
- Computer and printer
- Flat paintbrushes
- Blue painter's tape
- Freezer paper

HOW TO

1. Cut one 8½" × 11" piece of Stitch-N-Tear and place it onto freezer paper to protect underlying surfaces.

2. Paint the Stitch-N-Tear with acrylic paints, working with several colors while they are still wet so the paints will blend into each other, creating an uneven, yet smooth appearance. When done, allow it to dry completely.

3. Place the dry painted Stitch-N-Tear into the paper bed of your inkjet printer. Print an image from your computer onto the painted Stitch-N-Tear sheet.

Print image from computer.

4. Randomly rubber stamp designs on top of the printed image (see Stamping with Rubber Stamps, page 27). For more depth, overlap and layer the rubber-stamped images for extra visual appeal. Keep in mind that darker ink will be more visible on lighter paint colors and printed designs. Spray the Stitch-N-Tear with workable fixative. Let dry, then apply 1 to 2 coats of liquid varnish.

Rubber stamp image onto printed Stitch-N-Tear.

VARIATION

Repeat the steps for computer printing to create another layer of design. Simply feed the printed Stitch-N-Tear image through the printer again for additional images. When inkjet printing onto Stitch-N-Tear, tape the top and bottom to a sheet of white, all-purpose printer paper to prevent it from jamming in the printer.

5. Use paper punches to cut shapes from the Stitch-N-Tear, or tear it with your hands or with decorative-edge metal rulers.

Cut with paper punch.

Or tear with ruler.

TISSUE FABRIC

Postcard with tissue fabric base

I love collecting tissue papers from my purchases and then recycling them to create my own unique fabric. Once created, tissue fabric makes a great mixed-media element that can be used as a quilt substrate or as an embellishment layer.

MATERIALS

- Tissue papers or 1-ply paper napkins (printed and plain)
- Muslin
- Double-sided fusible web (Steam-A-Seam 2)
- Angelina and Crystalina fibers
- Acrylic paints (Golden Fluid Acrylics)
- Parchment paper or pressing cloth
- Flat paintbrush
- Iron
- Freezer paper
- Foil (optional)
- Cheesecloth (optional)
- Rubber stamps (optional)
- Board book (optional)

HOW TO

1. Peel the backing paper from one side of a piece of double-sided fusible web.

2. Apply torn pieces of tissue papers to the sticky side of the fusible web. Completely fill the piece of web, overlapping the edges. To ensure that the iron does not get adhesive on it, cover the tissue with parchment paper or a pressing cloth; press.

Apply tissue to one side of fusible web.

3. Peel the backing from a second piece of fusible web and fuse it to the top of the tissue paper.

4. Remove the second backing sheet from the fusible web that you applied on top of the tissue paper in Step 3. Apply Angelina and Crystalina fibers onto this sheet of the fusible web. Cover the surface with parchment paper and iron.

Apply Angelina and Crystalina fibers.

5. Paint this new surface with diluted acrylic paints. Fluid paints are highly pigmented; diluting the acrylic paint allows the sparkle of the Angelina fibers to show through. Start diluting with 1 part water to 1 part acrylic paint and adjust ratios until the desired effect is achieved.

Paint tissue with acrylics.

6. Remove the fusible web backing from underneath the first layer of tissue fabric. Place the sticky side down onto the muslin. Cover the tissue with parchment paper and iron, fusing the tissue to the muslin.

Peel tissue from backing film.

![flower] **VARIATIONS**

※ Apply painted cheesecloth in Step 2 for added texture.

※ Add rubber-stamped images onto the finished tissue fabric (see Stamping with Rubber Stamps, page 27).

※ Add foil after applying a second layer of the double-sided fusible web and removing its second backing layer. Because the tissue fabric is slightly sticky, foil can be applied by placing it shiny-side up onto the tissue. Iron the foil randomly onto the tissue with the edge of the iron. The trowel point attachment of the Creative Textile Tool (see page 12) can also be used to apply foil. Be sure to use parchment paper placed on top of the fusible web to protect your iron.

Apply foil onto tissue fabric with iron.

※ Instead of fusing to muslin, iron the tissue fabric onto printed paper or a board book.

EASY MIXED-MEDIA PATCHWORK FABRIC

Postcard with easy mixed-media patchwork fabric base, Angelina heart, and painted fast2fuse

I love this technique because it uses up all of the fabric scraps left over from other projects. The finished fabric is quite durable. The matte medium acts as an adhesive, keeping the patchwork fabric flexible without the need for a base fabric to stabilize it. The patchwork, even without painting and the addition of tissue, is still a wonderful creation.

Geometric shapes (dots, diamonds, and circles) and text stamps work well for this technique. The finished mixed-media fabric can be used as a background, die-cut, punched, or freely cut and used as an embellishment or as a traditional fabric. For extra texture and detail, machine or hand embroidery can be added.

MATERIALS
- Fabric (small pieces cut into irregular shapes)
- Tissue paper, solid and with printed designs (optional)
- Matte medium (Liquitex)
- Pigment inkpads, 2–3 colors suitable for fabric
- Metallic acrylic paints, 2–3 colors (Lumiere by Jacquard or Fluid Acrylics by Golden)
- Colorless Extender (Jacquard)
- Rubber and foam stamps
- Flat paintbrush
- Decorative-edge fabric scissors
- Freezer paper

HOW TO

1. Use decorative-edge scissors to cut the fabric into various irregular shapes.

2. Use a paintbrush to apply a thin coat of matte medium to the shiny side of the freezer paper. Place the cut fabric pieces right side up on the freezer paper and apply matte medium on top of them.

Plain patchwork

3. While the matte medium is still wet, randomly apply torn tissue paper on top of the fabric patchwork. Leave some of the areas of the patchwork blank.

Apply tissue on patchwork.

4. To create a more transparent color, dilute acrylic paint with 2 parts Colorless Extender to 1 part acrylic paint. Paint this mixture onto the fabric and tissue patchwork. Use at least 2 colors of acrylic paint and let it dry completely.

5. Stamp the patchwork with inked rubber and foam stamps (see Stamping with Rubber Stamps, page 27, and Stamping with Foam Stamps, page 26). For added visual interest, use many different stamps and ink colors in overlapping layers.

Stamp patchwork with rubber and foam stamps.

> **TIP**
> "Waste not, want not." After removing the freezer paper, use it as painted paper for another project (see Creating Base Material: Paper, page 37).

> **TIP**
> Use your favorite stamps to custom design plain tissue paper. Use a solvent ink, such as StazOn, so the ink won't smear when the matte medium is applied to the patchwork.

SILK FUSION

Postcard with silk fusion base

Silk fusion bonds silk roving—in this case, silk hankies—together to create a new piece of silk. Because I love creating and designing my own fabrics, experimenting with silk hankies led me to this technique for silk fusion.

Once completed, this technique yields a thin, wispy piece of silk paperlike material that can then be rubber-stamped, sprayed with color, or cut into embellishments with scissors or a rotary cutter. It has a luminous quality that adds an ethereal texture to any fabric collage project.

Silk hankies tend to get snagged if you have rough spots on your hands—apply lotion before working with them.

MATERIALS

- Silk hankies, plain or dyed
- Watercolor spray paints, several colors (Radiant Rain Misters by LuminArte)
- Watercolor paint cakes (Twinkling H20s by LuminArte)
- Reinker bottles (Tim Holtz Distress Dye Reinker by Ranger Ink; optional)
- Pigment inkpad (Brilliance by Tsukineko)
- Spray fabric stiffener (Stiffen Stuff by Beacon)
- Rubber stamp
- Angelina fibers (optional)
- Adhesive granules (Bo-Nash Bonding Agent 007; optional)
- Round paintbrush (optional)
- Iron
- Parchment paper (2 sheets cut slightly larger than hankie)
- Cosmetic sponge

HOW TO

1. Gently pull one hankie apart into one thin layer.

2. Place the silk hankie on a piece of parchment paper.

3. Spray the hankie with the spray fabric stiffener until it is damp.

4. Cover the hankie with parchment paper and press with an iron on the silk setting. Turn over the parchment sandwich and iron the other side.

5. Pull away the layers of parchment paper to reveal the fused silk. Pull the silk off the parchment paper.

6. Spray the hankie with watercolor paints or paint watercolors on with a brush, using the technique for Painting fast2fuse with Watercolors, page 22. Let dry completely.

7. Rubber stamp the fused hankie with pigment ink.

Rubber stamp images onto fused silk.

Finished silk fusion

VARIATIONS

* After the hankie is fused together, apply a small amount of adhesive granules onto the silk and then add wisps of Angelina fibers. Cover with parchment paper and press quickly with an iron.

* Try using liquid from reinker bottles instead of watercolor paints. Simply blot the ink onto the fused hankie with a cosmetic sponge.

PAPER

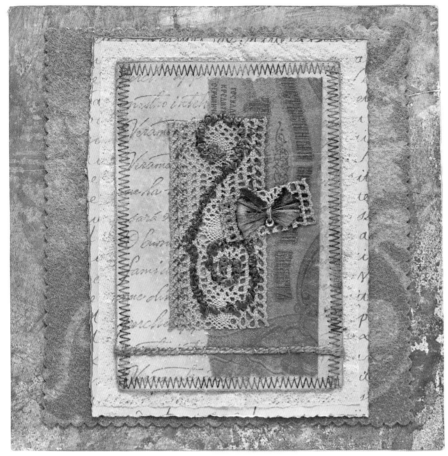

Book cover with "waste not, want not" paper base

I like to incorporate paper in my collage projects along with fabric. I paint, stamp, stencil, tear, stitch, foil, spray with metallic paint, and scrunch it for added texture.

Feel free to experiment—the sky's the limit.

MATERIALS

- Various papers (tissue paper, rice paper, watercolor paper, brown paper, parchment paper, scrapbook paper, freezer paper, wax paper)

- Acrylic or metallic acrylic paints (Golden Fluid Acrylics, Adirondack Dimensional Pearls by Ranger or Lumiere by Jacquard)

- Pigmented mica powder (Pearl Ex Pigment Powder by Jacquard)

- Pigment Inks (Brilliance by Tsukineko)

- Watercolor paints (Twinkling H20s or Radiant Rain Misters by LuminArte)

- Watermark inkpads

- Leafing pen (Krylon)

- Rubber and foam stamps

- Cosmetic sponge or paper towel

- Flat and round paintbrushes

- Stencils

- Paper towels

- Freezer paper

- Gesso (optional)

HOW TO

Here are various techniques for working with paper. The best option is to experiment with all of the papers and various paints, using the Painting and Stamping Techniques (pages 17–29), until you find appealing combinations. Additional creative suggestions follow.

- Paint tissue or rice paper with acrylic paints to create a delicate, shining accent that is great for embellishments and layers.

- Painted and torn watercolor paper makes a great substrate, or it can be placed behind embellishments for visual interest. Sponge or blot the painted watercolor paper with a paper towel and add additional layers of color with acrylic paints. Finish the torn edges with a leafing pen.

- Brown lunch or paper grocery bags turn into beautiful papers when painted with watercolors. After painting, stamp the surface with a watermark inkpad and apply pigment powders for quick, easy custom-designed paper.

- Recycle the freezer or wax paper used to protect your work surface in previous techniques. Stamp, dry brush, or stencil it with what I call the "waste not, want not" technique. Paper towels saved from project cleanup are also great to incorporate into any collage project. The base of the book cover bottom layer on this page is made from recycled paper.

- Paint scrapbook papers with diluted acrylic paints or gesso and stamp them with pigment inks.

- Tear the painted paper, reassemble it, and stitch it together to create a paper patchwork.

NONTRADITIONAL PATCHWORK FABRIC

Postcard with nontraditional patchwork fabric base

I use this technique to create a fabric collage base for my projects. In addition to being great for art quilts, this technique works well for any fabric project.

MATERIALS

- Fabric scraps
- Fabric, felt, or batting cut into a square or rectangle (use as base fabric)
- Double-sided fusible web (Steam-A-Seam 2)
- Decorative machine thread
- Disappearing fabric marker
- Scissors
- Iron
- Sewing machine with free-motion embroidery foot

HOW TO

1. Tear fabric scraps into the desired size pieces.

2. Peel the backing from one side of the fusible web and iron it onto the wrong side of the torn fabric pieces.

3. Cut your fabric base to the desired size and shape.

4. Peel off the remaining backing from the fusible web scraps.

5. Arrange the fabric scrap pieces onto the base fabric, place parchment paper on top, and fuse in place following the manufacturer's instructions. Overlap the pieces to create a patchwork composition.

Arrange fabric scrap pieces.

 TIP

When finished, the fabric collage can be used as is or as an additional layer of embellishment. Hand embroidery and couched fibers can also be added for extra texture.

6. Machine zigzag around the edges of the patchwork. Use 2 to 4 different colors of thread to randomly stitch the edges.

Machine zigzag stitch around fabric.

7. Use a disappearing marker to draw shapes, such as hearts, swirls, or circles, directly onto additional fabric scraps for the patchwork.

Draw shapes with disappearing marker.

8. Set up your sewing machine for free-motion embroidery. Stitch doodle onto the drawn lines. Cover the rest of the patchwork with random freestyle stitching.

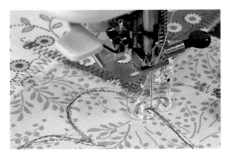

Free-motion stitch onto patchwork.

9. Set your sewing machine back to straight stitching. Randomly machine stitch straight lines onto the patchwork.

FREE-FORM SCRAP FABRIC

Postcard with free-form scrap fabric base

This technique uses up all the leftover scraps from previous techniques described in this book. Project waste can be turned into multicolored materials and incorporated into any project. Because this technique is very free-form, the scraps can be any shape or size, depending on how you would like to use them. I like to use the created material as a background behind embellishments, or it can stand alone as a completed collage unto itself.

MATERIALS

- Scraps from previous techniques (for example, fabric, lace, trim, paper, Lutradur, fast2fuse)
- Felt or other fabric (for the base)
- Decorative thread
- Double-sided fusible web (Steam-A-Seam 2)
- Repositionable spray craft adhesive
- Scissors
- Parchment paper
- Iron
- Sewing machine

HOW TO

1. Peel the backing from one side of the fusible web.

2. Cut and arrange the scraps on the sticky side of the web. **Note:** Some of the pieces, such as embossed velvet and crayon muslin pieces, will need to be added after the initial pressing.

Arrange scraps onto fusible web.

3. Place parchment paper on top of the scraps. Fuse in place with an iron, following the manufacturer's instructions. Allow the fabric to cool before removing the parchment paper.

4. Peel off the remaining fusible web backing from the back side of the scrap fabric layer. Place it sticky side down onto the base fabric. Cover with parchment and press with an iron.

5. Use repositionable spray craft adhesive to adhere the backs of the elements, such as embossed velvet, that would not iron down.

6. Machine stitch doodle randomly on top of the scrap fabric to secure all the elements to the base fabric.

Finished scrap fabric

creating texture

Texture adds dimension.

Texture adds both a visual and a tactile layer to your artwork and can be the difference between a plain piece of art and a stunning piece of art. I like to add dimension to my artwork whenever possible. The following techniques are some of my favorite ways to do this.

NEEDLE FELTING

Postcard with needle-felted organza fabric

Whether you use a needle-punch machine or the handheld Clover tool, your results will be unique every time. I like to create needle-felted fabric and use it as a base for quilts or Artist Trading Cards (ATCs). I also cut it into embellishments. Painting the organza first adds a shimmering layer to the material; adding cheesecloth creates even more texture.

MATERIALS
- Batting (Nature-fil Bamboo by Fairfield) or felt
- Organza
- Watercolor-painted organza ribbon and fabric (similar to Painting fast2fuse with Watercolors, page 22)
- Diluted acrylic-painted cheesecloth (similar to Layered Painting and Stamping on Muslin, page 28)
- Acrylic-painted dryer sheets (see Lutradur and Dryer Sheets, page 68)
- Metallic acrylic paints (Lumiere by Jacquard; optional)
- Repositionable spray craft adhesive

- Needle-felting embellisher machine or felting needles and brush mat (Clover)
- Flat paintbrush or stencil brush (optional)
- Iron
- Scissors
- Parchment paper

HOW TO
1. Spray one side of the batting with repositionable spray adhesive and layer the dryer sheets onto it randomly.

2. Cover the dryer sheets with a combination of organza, painted organza, and painted cheesecloth.

Cover dryer sheets with organza and cheesecloth.

3. Needle felt through all layers with a needle-felting machine or felting needles with a brush mat underneath. The sharp, barbed needles will pull and secure all the layers together to create a unique, even fabric.

Needle felt layers together.

4. Cover the fabric with parchment paper and press with an iron.

5. Cut the completed needle-felted organza fabric into shapes. Use as appliqué pieces or as the base for a postcard or quilt project.

Completed felted organza and cut shapes

 **VARIATION**

After pressing, dry brush (page 18) or stencil acrylic paint onto the fabric (see Stenciling with Paint, page 17). Stitch doodle for added embellishment (page 43).

Other needle-felted fabrics

SOLVRON

Solvron-textured and painted silk fabric

Many different looks can be achieved using Solvron, a hot water-soluble fabric. I like using this technique as an embellishment or as a layer to give my work added visual interest.

MATERIALS

- Silk, felt, or velvet for base fabric
- Hot-water-soluble stabilizer (Solvron)
- Repositionable craft spray adhesive
- Spray bottle filled with hot water
- Scissors
- Sewing machine and thread

HOW TO

1. Spray the wrong side of the base fabric with repositionable craft spray.

2. Cut a piece of Solvron the same size as the fabric and apply it to the sticky side of the fabric.

3. Machine stitch the Solvron side of the fabric, using any kind of stitch. Stitching can be in even rows or in a random, decorative pattern. If the stitches are placed close together, a more densely textured fabric will result after hot water is applied.

Machine stitch fabric.

4. Lightly mist the Solvron side of the fabric with hot water. The Solvron will start to shrink, causing the fabric to pucker and create interesting texture. Do not completely remove the Solvron; instead, start with a light mist and add more if you want a more puckered, interesting effect. The resulting textured fabric can be used as a layer or an embellishment.

 VARIATIONS

* For added design, apply hand embroidery to the textured fabric.

* Stamp designs onto the silk or felt and let it dry before attaching it to the Solvron. This will add extra design elements to your finished piece (see the stamped silk collage on canvas, page 77).

STITCH DOODLING FREE-MOTION EMBROIDERY

Postcards with stitch doodling

I call this technique *stitch doodling* because it is like pencil doodling but with a sewing machine and thread. This technique adds texture, color, and interest to my artwork. I find it helpful to use a disappearing fabric marker to first map out where I want the doodles to be placed. It is important to read your sewing machine's manual for setting up the free-motion embroidery and to practice on a separate piece of fabric to get the feel of free-motion work.

MATERIALS

- Fabric scraps, small to medium in size
- Tearaway fabric stabilizer (Stitch-N-Tear; optional)
- Scissors
- Sewing machine with free-motion capability
- Darning foot
- Disappearing fabric marker (optional)
- Hoop (optional)

HOW TO

1. Set up your sewing machine for free-motion sewing and attach a darning foot. A fabric stabilizer and hoop may be necessary to ensure stability of the fabric. I do not use a stabilizer when I use a heavy fabric, felt, or layered fabric.

2. Practice stitching by slowly moving the fabric. Doodle or draw designs onto the fabric with the sewing machine thread. The design can be freely stitched. Or you can predraw a design onto the fabric with a disappearing marker and trace over the lines with sewing machine thread.

Examples of doodled stitches

DECORATIVE MACHINE STITCHES

Decorative machine stitches

The two most common stitches that come on sewing machines are the straight stitch and the zigzag stitch. Both are versatile, and both can be used to add texture, color, and another layer of design. Even the most inexpensive sewing machines come with at least one or two decorative stitches. These decorative stitches can be used anywhere (for example, to decorate fabric for making beads) and are easily added wherever a little more design is needed.

THREAD FABRIC

Postcard with thread fabric

Thread fabric is created with free-motion embroidery stitched onto dissolvable water-soluble stabilizers. The thread can be stitched down extremely overlapped and dense, or it can be added more lightly for an open, lacey look—any way you want it! Once I create a piece of thread fabric, I often paint it with spray watercolors.

MATERIALS

- Water-soluble stabilizer (Super Solvy)
- Scissors
- Sewing machine thread (100% cotton was used here.)
- Sewing machine

HOW TO

1. Cut the water-soluble stabilizer to the desired finished size.

2. Set up the sewing machine for free-motion embroidery.

3. Free-motion stitch onto the stabilizer. Cover the entire piece with thread in a meandering fashion. Be sure to cross over previous stitching lines so that when the stabilizer is washed away, you are left with a cohesive piece of thread fabric.

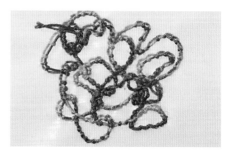

Free-motion stitch onto stabilizer.

Completely cover stabilizer with thread stitches.

4. Following the manufacturer's directions, dissolve the stabilizer in water to leave a threadlike fabric. Let dry.

Finished thread fabric

embellishments

This collage of embellishments is an example of how beads, buttons, altered lace, and ribbons can be used for artwork.

Embellishments are like the cherry on top of ice cream! Adding embellishments is my favorite part of the creative process. When you design and create your own beads, ribbons, and button embellishments, they add a completely unique and personal element to your work that gives it a one-of-a-kind touch.

PAPER BUTTONS

Paper buttons

I like making these quick paper buttons. The vinyl protects the paper and can be used as is or colored with alcohol inks.

MATERIALS

■ Quilter's Vinyl (C&T Publishing)

■ Double-sided fusible web (Steam-A-Seam 2)

■ Double-sided decorative paper

■ Alcohol ink (Ranger Adirondack Ink)

■ Decorative-edge scissors

■ Flat paintbrush

■ Paper hole punch

■ Circle paper punches

■ Parchment paper

■ Disappearing fabric marker

■ Scissors

■ Iron

■ Paper towel

HOW TO

1. Decide how many and what size buttons you want to make. Cut off enough Quilter's Vinyl to fold and cover both sides of the buttons you will be making.

2. Cut a piece of double-sided fusible web the same size as the Quilter's Vinyl piece. Remove one layer of backing paper and fuse it to the Quilter's Vinyl.

3. Remove the second layer of backing paper from the fusible web.

4. Punch or cut various-sized circles from decorative paper.

5. Place the circles on one side of the Quilter's Vinyl (against the fusible web) and fold the vinyl over the circles so they are sandwiched between two vinyl layers. Cover with parchment paper and press with an iron.

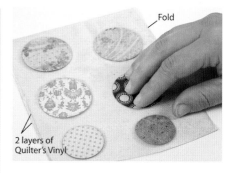

Circles sandwiched in folded vinyl

6. Remove the parchment paper and let the vinyl cool.

7. Cut around the circles with decorative-edge scissors.

Trim around circles.

8. Paint the buttons with alcohol ink to add a transparent color to the buttons. Add and subtract ink by applying and blotting ink with a paper towel until the desired color is achieved.

Paint buttons.

9. Use a disappearing fabric marker to mark 2 dots at the center of each button.

10. Use a paper hole punch to create 2 holes at the marked dots.

ALTERED LACE

Altered lace

I alter lace by dyeing it with ink and then attaching it to my artwork with embroidery stitches. Altered lace can be used alone or layered behind another embellishment, such as metal jewelry findings. Dyeing the lace yourself gives you the ability to coordinate the colors specifically for your artwork.

MATERIALS

- Lace or doilies
- Liquid dye ink, 1 or more colors (Tim Holtz Distress Ink Reinkers by Ranger)
- Watercolor spray paint (Radiant Rain Misters by LuminArte; optional)
- Flat paintbrush
- Spray bottle filled with water
- Embroidery thread
- Hand sewing needle
- Sewing machine

HOW TO

1. Mist the lace with water.

2. Mix the liquid dye ink with water. The amount of water added will determine how light or dark the resulting lace color will be. I find that a 50/50 ratio is a good place to start.

3. Apply the diluted ink onto the lace with a paintbrush and let the lace dry completely. The color does not have to be even to create a lovely effect.

Apply diluted ink onto lace.

 TIP

Radiant Rain Misters by LuminArte work equally well and provide an intense metallic color when applied to the lace or doilies. Another design possibility is to embroider the lace by machine or by hand (see Decorative Machine Stitches, page 44).

ALTERED RIBBON

Altered ribbon

Altered ribbon is a very versatile element of design. Any ribbon can be used, and the amount of alteration is entirely up to you. I like to add lots of tissue and stamped layers to my ribbon, but not so much that it becomes too bulky.

MATERIALS

- Ribbon, any kind
- Tissue paper
- Double-sided fusible web (Steam-A-Seam 2)
- Scissors
- Parchment paper
- Iron
- Embroidery thread (optional)
- Hand sewing needle (optional)
- Sewing machine (optional)
- Rubber stamps (optional)
- Pigment inkpads, several colors (optional)
- Cosmetic sponges (optional)

HOW TO

1. Cut a strip of double-sided fusible web to the exact width and length of the ribbon. Remove one backing layer from the web and heat-press the web to the right side of the ribbon. Let cool before removing the other backing from the web.

2. Partially cover the sticky side of the ribbon with torn tissue papers.

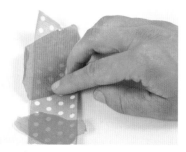

Apply torn tissue paper.

3. Cover the ribbon with parchment paper and press with an iron.

4. If you like, randomly rubber stamp the ribbon with images. Or apply ink with cosmetic sponges.

TIP

Use altered ribbon as the focal point or embellishment layer for postcards, ATCs, or small quilts. For added embellishment, hand or machine embroider designs over altered ribbon.

FELT BEADS

Felt beads are versatile and can be used for adornment of jewelry and fabric projects.

I like the simplicity of this bead-making technique. It is a good way to use up leftover scraps of felt from other projects. I have found that creating beads is addicting. Beads are the perfect embellishment for any mixed-media artwork. I make beads in batches so that I have them on hand whenever I feel inspired to add them to my artwork.

MATERIALS

- Felt
- Watercolor spray paints (Radiant Rain Misters by LuminArte)
- Contrasting or metallic thread
- Fabric adhesive (Fabri-Tac by Beacon)
- Flat paintbrush (optional)
- Straight and decorative-edge fabric scissors
- ¼"-diameter dowel or pencil (Inner diameter will determine size of finished bead.)
- Sewing machine with decorative stitches
- Wire and crystals (optional)
- Leafing pens (optional)
- Liquid varnish

HOW TO

1. Machine stitch lines of decorative stitches onto the felt.

2. Use decorative-edge scissors to cut the felt next to the decorative stitches.

Trim edges of felt with decorative-edge scissors.

3. Cut the machine-stitched felt strips into 1½˝ lengths. The final length of the strip will be determined by the dowel size used to create the bead (see Step 5). In this project, I used a ¼˝ dowel.

4. Spray the felt strips with watercolors. Set aside to dry completely.

5. Wrap a dried decorated felt strip around a dowel into a bead shape. Secure the ends with fabric adhesive.

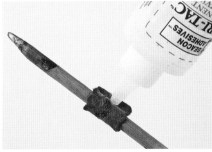

Secure bead shape with fabric adhesive.

6. When the bead is dry, remove it from the dowel and apply a coat of liquid varnish.

VARIATIONS

* Beads do not have to be painted. Other options include using beautiful metallic machine embroidery threads when stitching, wrapping the beads with wire and crystals, or edging the beads with leafing pens.

* Try diluted acrylic paints instead of watercolors for a different look. Use the machine-stitched and painted felt strips as layered embellishments.

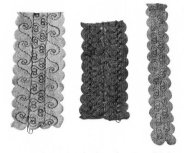

Use machine-stitched and painted felt strips as embellishment.

FELTED ORGANZA AND SILK BEADS

Organza beads

Even the tiniest organza and silk scrap pieces can be turned into lovely bead embellishments.

MATERIALS

- Needle-felted organza or silk (see Needle Felting, page 41)

- Acrylic paint (Lumiere by Jacquard; optional)

- Dye-Na-Flow (Jacquard; optional)

- Decorative fibers or yarn (such as those included in YLI Painters Potpourri Packs; optional)

- Spray fabric stiffener (Stiffen Stuff by Beacon)

- Fabric adhesive (Fabri-Tac by Beacon)

- ¼˝-diameter dowel or pencil (Size will determine inner diameter of finished bead.)

- Leafing pen (Krylon; optional)

- Drinking straw (optional)

- Rubber stamp (optional)

- Beads and decorative metal pieces (optional)

HOW TO

1. Choose the desired width for your bead. Cut needle-felted organza or silk into strips of this width.

2. Wrap the strips around a dowel or pencil. Secure the ends with fabric adhesive.

3. Spray the fabric-wrapped dowel or pencil with fabric stiffener. As the fabric dries, occasionally move the bead on the dowel to prevent it from sticking. When dry, remove the bead from the dowel.

4. Wrap the fabric bead with decorative fibers and/or contrasting strips of needle-felted organza. For added embellishment, hand stitch or glue small beads and decorative metal pieces to the organza bead.

3. Paint several coats of clear gloss medium onto the paper bead. Let the bead dry between each coat.

PAPER BEADS

Paper beads

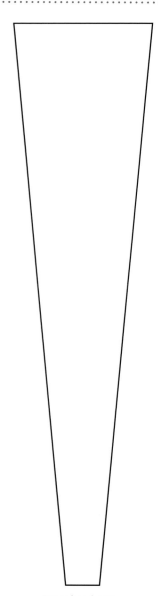

Paper bead pattern

Paper beads are versatile and easy to make. You can use them to adorn both fabric and paper projects. Once created, use them to embellish quilts, jewelry, or books.

MATERIALS
- Decorative cardstock or handmade paper
- Tissue paper (optional)
- Fibers (such as threads or yarn included in YLI Painters Potpourri Packs; optional)
- Clear gloss medium (Ranger Inkssentials Glossy Accents)
- Paper adhesive (Zip Dry by Beacon)
- Dowel rod or pencil (Size will determine inner diameter of finished bead.)
- Small, flat paintbrush
- Drawing pencil
- Scissors
- Rubber stamps (optional)
- Metal findings (optional)

HOW TO
1. Lightly trace the paper bead pattern onto a piece of decorative paper. Cut out the pattern along the traced line, then erase the line.

2. Roll the paper onto the dowel and secure it with paper adhesive.

fibers and hand
embroidery

Examples of fibers and a sampler of stitches showing how embroidery can be incorporated into a fabric art piece.

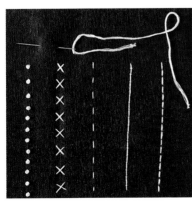

Hand embroidery stitch examples

Fibers such as yarn, floss, metallic threads, and cord make a great layer of embellishment for mixed-media projects. I like to wrap fibers around beads for added ornamentation. Hand embroidery stitches are also great for tacking and securing embellishments onto a project, such as a quilt.

SILK CARRIER ROD WASTE

Artist Trading Card (ATC) with decorative machine stitching on silk carrier rod waste and fibers

I love using silk carrier rod waste as an embellishment. These silk carrier rods are the by-product of creating spun silk. You can use the rods as is or mist them with water and iron them between parchment papers for a flat surface.

MATERIALS

■ Silk carrier rod waste (YLI)

■ Decorative fibers or yarn (such as those included in YLI's Painters Potpourri Packs)

■ Spray bottle filled with water

■ Parchment paper

■ Polyester sewing machine thread

■ Iron

■ Hand embroidery needle

■ Sewing machine

HOW TO

1. Gently unfold the silk carrier rod waste, mist lightly with water, cover with parchment paper, and press with an iron on the silk setting.

Unfold silk carrier rod waste.

2. Machine or hand embroider designs onto the flattened silk rod, using polyester sewing machine thread or decorative fibers or yarns.

3. Use the finished piece as an embellishment or as a focal point for a small project such as an ATC or postcard.

PLUS-SIZE INCHIES

Canvas board with Inchies embellished with beads, jewelry findings, and buttons

Inchies are 1″ mixed-media squares that can be used as an embellishment, jewelry element, or when a little extra "something" is needed to complete your design. "Plus-size" Inchies are 1½″-square and are the size that I most often create.

MATERIALS

- fast2fuse, 8½″ × 11″ sheet (C&T Publishing)

- Organza inkjet-printable fabric, 1 sheet (ExtravOrganza by Jacquard)

- Tissue paper, assorted colors

- Printable images (such as those from The Vintage Workshop)

- Dye-Na-Flow paint, 2–3 colors (Jacquard)

- Metallic acrylic paint (Lumiere by Jacquard)

- Pigment inkpads

- Granular adhesive (Bo-Nash 007 Bonding Agent)

- Spray bottle filled with water

- Rubber stamps, including script and dots

- Cosmetic sponge

- Scissors

- Rotary cutter, ruler, and mat

- Computer and inkjet printer

- Iron

- Parchment paper

HOW TO

1. Paint an 8½″ × 11″ sheet of fast2fuse with Dye-Na-Flow mixed with acrylic paint (see page 23).

Painted fast2fuse

2. Rubber stamp images onto tissue paper with pigment inkpads. Cut or tear the tissue paper into geometric shapes such as squares. Randomly place the tissue pieces onto the painted fast2fuse, cover with parchment paper, and press with an iron.

3. Following the manufacturer's instructions, print images onto organza inkjet-printable fabric. Cut the printed fabric into randomly sized pieces.

Cut printed organza inkjet-printable fabric.

4. Apply adhesive bonding granules onto the tissue paper pieces. Place the organza inkjet-printed fabric pieces onto the fast2fuse, randomly covering the tissue papers. Cover the fast2fuse with parchment paper and press with an iron.

Apply adhesive bonding granules to tissue pieces.

5. Use a cosmetic sponge to randomly apply acrylic paint onto the surface.

6. Add more rubber-stamped images directly onto your surface.

7. Randomly stitch doodle the surface (see Stitch Doodling Free-Motion Embroidery, page 43).

Randomly stitch doodle surface.

8. Use a rotary cutter, ruler, and mat to cut the fast2fuse into 1½″ × 11″ strips.

9. Machine zigzag along the long side edges of each strip.

Machine zigzag long edges.

10. Cut the strips into 1½″ squares. Zigzag stitch along the unstitched side of the square.

VARIATIONS

✳ Make Nontraditional Patchwork Fabric (page 38) and use it to create "plus-size" Inchies. Follow Steps 8–10 for finishing the edges. Use these "plus-size" Inchies as fun embellishments.

✳ Instead of cutting into strips, use the full sheet uncut as a background or base for an art quilt or ATC.

Nontraditional patchwork fabric "plus-size" Inchies

Uncut Inchies sheet applied to a wood frame

hot tools

Hot tools

I have been experimenting with hot tools for quite some time and am still finding new and interesting ways to use them. Hot tools, such as the Creative Textile Tool by Walnut Hollow, and heat-embossing tools provide many creative options for making unique mixed-media embellishments, backgrounds, and layers. I love to experiment by cutting, etching, hot stamping, and embossing painted fabrics and papers to give them another element of design.

It is important when using hot tools to follow the manufacturer's safety instructions and precautions. When using hot tools with synthetic materials, such as fast-2fuse, painted felt, canvas, craft foam, Lutradur, and Tyvek, it is important to work in a well-ventilated area and use a respirator or mask. Pigment and embossing powders can become airborne, so a mask should also be worn when using them.

EMBOSSED VELVET

Embossed velvet using vintage lace doily

Lift velvet to reveal embossed image.

Stamped and embossed velvet

Embossing velvet is a simple technique that yields beautiful results every time. The embossed design can be used as a background or embellishment. Using alternative materials, such as lace, opens up endless design possibilities!

MATERIALS

- Rayon/acetate velvet
- Vintage lace (optional)
- Metallic color pigment inkpad (Tsukineko Brilliance)
- Spray bottle filled with water
- Deep-etched rubber stamp
- Iron

HOW TO

1. Load a deep-etched rubber stamp with pigment ink (see Stamping with Rubber Stamps, page 27).

2. Place velvet, plush side down, onto the stamp.

3. Lightly mist the back of the velvet with water.

4. Set the iron to the cotton setting and press the back of the velvet. Hold for 5–10 seconds. Remove the iron and lift the velvet to reveal your embossed design.

VARIATION

Use found items, such as vintage lace, instead of a rubber stamp. Place the raised design side of the lace face down onto the velvet, mist lightly with water, and press with the iron. The heat will transfer the design. Lift the lace to reveal the embossed design.

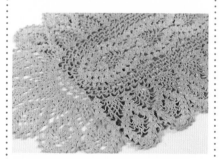

Place lace face down on nap side of velvet.

Lift lace to reveal embossed design.

ETCHED VELVET

Acrylic stenciled postcards with etched design

This technique inspires lots of creativity in my artwork. Because my drawing skills are not the greatest, I frequently doodle or draw freehand designs. Doodling these designs onto velvet is addicting and fun.

MATERIALS

▦ Rayon/acetate velvet

▦ Watercolor spray paints, 2 colors (Radiant Rain Misters by LuminArte)

▦ Acrylic paint (Lumiere by Jacquard)

▦ Creative Textile Tool (Walnut Hollow)

▦ Stencil (optional)

▦ Tempered glass, heat-resistant mat (Walnut Hollow)

▦ Blue painter's tape

▦ Wire brush

▦ Paper towels

HOW TO

1. Heat the Creative Textile Tool with the Long Mini Flow Point attached and work on a heat-resistant surface.

2. Tape the velvet onto a glass mat, nap side up.

3. Etch a freehand design, such as swirls or doodles, directly onto the nap side of the velvet.

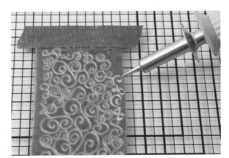

Etch design onto velvet.

4. Place the etched velvet onto a protected surface. Spray watercolors randomly onto the velvet and blot with more paper towels.

Spray watercolors onto etched velvet.

VARIATION

Stencil designs onto velvet with acrylic paint. While the paint is still wet, use the Creative Textile Tool with the Tapered Point attached to etch around the perimeter and within the stenciled image.

Etch design onto a stenciled, acrylic paint design.

TIP

Keep the points of the Creative Textile Tool clean by frequently brushing them with a wire brush.

EMBOSSED BATTING

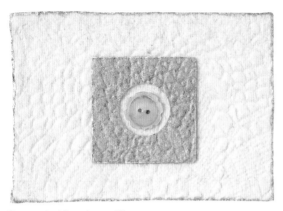

Postcard with embossed batting

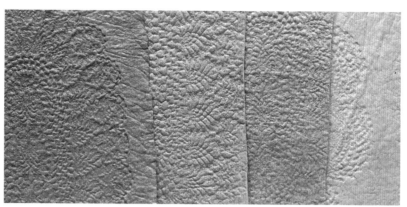

Batting embossed with doily and painted

Quilt batting is a staple that every quilter has on hand. It is traditionally used as the middle layer between the quilt top and backing. Embossing batting with lace or doilies takes this medium to a whole new level of creativity. Embossed batting makes a great base for any project, such as book covers, art quilts, or ATCs. It can also be cut into an embellishment.

MATERIALS

- Batting (Nature-fil Bamboo by Fairfield Processing Corporation)
- Doily or lace
- Textile medium (Fabric Painting Medium by Deco Art)
- Watercolor spray paints (Radiant Rain Misters by LuminArte; optional)
- Fabric spray paint (Simply Spray by Deval; optional)
- Fabric dye (tan color Rit Dye; optional)
- Water
- Spray bottle
- Parchment paper
- Scissors
- Iron

HOW TO

1. Cut a piece of batting slightly larger than the lace or doily.

2. Mix 1 part textile medium with 1 part water. Pour the mixture into a spray bottle.

3. Place the batting onto the parchment paper and mist it with the diluted textile medium. The batting should be moist but not saturated.

4. Place the lace onto the misted batting.

5. Cover the lace with parchment paper. At this point, the batting and lace should be sandwiched between 2 pieces of parchment paper. With an iron set to the cotton setting, press the parchment paper, ironing firmly onto the batting. Turn the parchment/batting over and press again.

6. Remove the parchment paper. Gently pull the lace from the batting to reveal an embossed lace image.

Gently pull lace from batting.

7. Spray the embossed batting with diluted tan fabric dye for a vintage look.

VARIATION

After embossing the batting, spray it with watercolor spray paints (see LuminArte, page 9), diluted acrylic paint poured into a spray bottle, or fabric spray paint.

Embossed, painted batting

EMBOSSED CRAFT FOAM

Artist Trading Card with embossed craft foam heart

MATERIALS

- Craft foam
- Metallic acrylic paint (Lumiere by Jacquard)
- Deep-etched rubber stamp
- Flat paintbrush
- Scissors
- Iron

HOW TO

1. Press an iron, set at the cotton setting, onto the craft foam for 5–7 seconds.

2. Lift the iron and immediately press a deep-etched rubber stamp onto the heated craft foam. Let cool.

Press stamp onto warm craft foam.

3. Remove the stamp. Paint the embossed craft foam with acrylic paint. Let it dry completely.

4. Trim around the embossed image to the desired size.

I like using craft foam because it is inexpensive and versatile. Not only can it become a great embellishment, but it also can be used as a foundation for any mixed-media project. Try embossing a whole sheet and using that as the background for your next art quilt.

EMBOSSED ANGELINA OR CRYSTALINA

Artist Trading Card with Angelina embellishment

There are many options when using Angelina and Crystalina fibers. I like to emboss the fibers with a rubber stamp to create a wispy, fabriclike embellishment. Once embossed, Angelina fibers can be cut into shapes free hand or—for more precise shapes—with a metal cookie cutter or stencil.

MATERIALS

- Fusible Angelina or Crystalina fibers
- Pigment inkpad (Tsukineko Brilliance)
- Rubber stamp
- Scissors
- Iron
- Parchment paper
- Cookie cutter or stencil (optional)

- Creative Textile Tool (Walnut Hollow; optional)
- Tempered glass, heat-resistant mat (Walnut Hollow; optional)

HOW TO

1. Ink the rubber stamp with the pigment inkpad.

2. Place a small amount of Angelina fibers onto the stamp and cover it with parchment paper.

Place fusible Angelina fibers onto rubber stamp and cover with parchment paper.

3. Very briefly (approximately 1–2 seconds) press the parchment paper with the hot iron set at the cotton setting.

4. Remove the parchment paper and lift the fused Angelina fibers from the rubber stamp.

Remove embossed Angelina from rubber stamp.

 VARIATIONS

* Angelina fibers can be cut into freehand shapes. For more precise shapes, use the Creative Textile Tool with its Tapered Point or use a cookie cutter or stencil. The cut design can be used as an embellishment or collage layer.

* Fused Angelina can also be cut into strips or squares with a rotary cutter, mat, and ruler.

Creating an Angelina embellishment

Cutting Angelina embellishment with stencil

FUSED ANGELINA OR CRYSTALINA

Postcard with needle-felted organza fabric layer and heart embellishment of Angelina

Fusing Angelina or Crystalina fibers onto painted fast2fuse is a quick way to add another layer to your design. Once Angelina is fused, it can be cut using the Creative Textile Tool, die-cut into shapes, or used as a background for small projects such as ATCs.

MATERIALS

- Watercolor-painted fast2fuse (see Painting fast2fuse with Watercolors, page 22)
- Fusible Angelina or Crystalina fibers
- Pigment inkpad (Tsukineko Brilliance)
- Rubber stamp with script design
- Parchment paper
- Iron

HOW TO

1. Place fast2fuse on parchment paper on a heat-resistant surface. Stamp watercolor-painted fast2fuse with a rubber stamp loaded with pigment ink (see Stamping with Rubber Stamps, page 27).

Stamp fast2fuse with script rubber stamp.

2. Place a thin layer of fusible Angelina fibers onto the fast2fuse.

3. Place parchment paper on top of the fusible Angelina fibers and press for 1 or 2 seconds with an iron.

Finished fast2fuse with Angelina fibers

ETCHED CANVAS

Postcard with etched canvas

Etching canvas with the Creative Textile Tool is a unique way to add texture and free-form design elements to your mixed-media projects. This technique can also be applied to canvas boards, which make a great base for artwork.

MATERIALS

- Canvas sheet pads (Fredrix Canvas Pads)

- Acrylic paints, 3 colors (Adirondack Dimensional Pearls by Ranger)

- Creative Textile Tool (Walnut Hollow)

- Cosmetic sponge

- Flat paintbrush

- Disappearing marker (optional)

- Freezer paper to protect underlying surfaces

- Tempered glass, heat-resistant mat (Walnut Hollow)

HOW TO

1. Paint a canvas sheet with several colors of acrylic paints. Overlap and blend the colors into each other while still wet for a mottled effect. Let dry.

2. Use the Creative Textile Tool on a heat-resistant glass mat with the Long Mini Flow Point attached to draw random designs, such as doodles and swirls, onto the painted canvas. Fill the entire canvas sheet with free-form designs. **Note:** You may want to use a disappearing marker to audition the design before actually etching it onto canvas.

Etch design onto painted canvas.

3. When you're finished doodling, sponge small areas of the etched canvas with acrylic paints.

Sponge acrylics onto etched canvas.

Use an inkjet printer to print photos or images onto computer canvas sheets, such as The Vintage Workshop Gloss Finish Artist Canvas Sheets. Repeat the directions on page 62 for etching onto canvas sheets but skip the painting steps.

Etch design onto inkjet canvas photo.

TIP

If a free-form design is not desirable or doesn't work with your overall design, use rubber-stamped images instead. Simply stamp the images onto the painted canvas with dye or solvent ink and trace over them with the Long Mini Flow Point attachment.

Painted board books from C&T can also be etched upon using the same technique.

EMBOSSING POWDERS ON BATTING

Postcard with embossing powders

I love bamboo batting because it is silky soft, accepts paint and dye, and has a beautiful sheen. Adding layers of embossing powders to the batting creates a unique embellishment that can easily be a focal point for any project.

MATERIALS

- Batting (Nature-fil Bamboo by Fairfield Processing Corporation)
- Paper or velvet, optional
- Dye-Na-Flow, 1 color (Jacquard)
- Metallic acrylic paints, 2-3 colors (Lumiere by Jacquard)
- Embossing powders, black and copper (as desired)
- Watermark stamp pad (VersaMark by Tsukineko)
- Foam stamp
- Craft tray
- Tempered glass, heat-resistant mat (Walnut Hollow)
- Tearaway stabilizer (Stitch-N-Tear; optional)
- Flat paintbrush
- Heat-embossing tool

HOW TO

1. Paint the batting with Dye-Na-Flow acrylic paint. Dry brush (page 18) the remaining colors onto the batting to add a small amount of additional color. Let dry.

2. Ink the stamp with the watermark inkpad and stamp the images onto the painted batting.

3. Working over a craft tray, shake copper embossing powder onto the stamped images. Shake off the excess into the tray.

Shake copper embossing powder onto watermark-stamped image.

4. Heat set the embossing powder with the heat tool on a tempered glass, heat-resistant mat. Position the tool approximately 6″ from the image and hold in place until the embossing powder turns shiny.

Heat set embossing powder.

5. Repeat Steps 2–4 using black embossing powder and stamping over the previous copper embossed image.

VARIATION

This technique also works great on Stitch-N-Tear, paper, and velvet.

Other example of embossing

ULTRA THICK EMBOSSING ENAMEL

Center heart, square, and roof edged with Ultra Thick Embossing Enamel

I like using Ultra Thick Embossing Enamel as a quick and easy way to finish the edges of my embellishments or fabric layers.

MATERIALS

- Painted fast2fuse with hot-stamped edges (see Painting fast-2fuse with Watercolors, page 22, and Hot Stamping, page 65)
- Ultra Thick Embossing Enamel (UTEE)
- Watermark inkpad (VersaMark by Tsukineko)
- Pigmented mica powder, 2–3 colors (Pearl Ex Pigment Powder by Jacquard)
- Round paintbrush
- Heat-embossing tool
- Tempered glass, heat-resistant mat (Walnut Hollow)
- Angelina fused to fast2fuse (optional)
- Tearaway stabilizer (Stitch-N-Tear; optional)
- Painted felt (optional)
- Leafing pen (Krylon; optional)
- Die-cutting machine (Sizzix; optional)
- Scissors

HOW TO

1. Use the die cut machine or scissors to cut painted fast2fuse into various shapes, such as frames or geometric shapes.

2. Press each edge of the cut fast-2fuse onto the watermark inkpad. Sprinkle a thick layer of UTEE on a paper plate or craft tray. Dip each edge into the UTEE and shake off the excess.

Ink edges with watermark inkpad.

3. Emboss the UTEE edges with a heat-embossing tool (page 64).

VARIATION

This technique also works well with painted felt, Angelina fused to fast2fuse, and Stitch-N-Tear. For a quick finished edge, use a gold or silver leafing pen instead of embossing enamel.

Other examples of finished edges

HOT STAMPING

Board book with hot-stamped embellishment on tag

Often, when heat is applied to synthetic fabric, it yields random, unexpected results. Hot stamping onto fabric is more uniform and controlled. I like to use this technique to finish the edges of embellishments. Adding foil makes a great design element, whether it is applied randomly to the fabric with an iron or cut into shapes.

MATERIALS
- Painted fast2fuse (see Painting fast2fuse with Watercolors, page 22)
- Pigment inkpad (Tsukineko Brilliance)
- Pigmented mica powder (Pearl Ex Pigment Powder by Jacquard)
- Foil
- Rubber stamp with script design
- Flat paintbrush
- Creative Textile Tool with Swirl and Trowel points (Walnut Hollow)
- Tempered glass, heat-resistant mat (Walnut Hollow)
- Die-cutting machine (Sizzix; optional)
- Scissors

HOW TO

1. Cut the painted fast2fuse to the desired shape and stamp it with a pigment-inked rubber stamp.

2. Use the Creative Textile Tool with the Swirl Point on a heat-resistant mat to hot stamp the edges.

Hot stamp edges with Swirl Point.

3. Brush the edges of the hot-stamped fast2fuse with pigmented mica powder.

Brush edges with pigmented mica powder.

4. Use scissors to cut a heart design from the foil. Place the foil heart shiny side up onto the fast2fuse.

5. Attach the Trowel Point to the Creative Textile Tool. Use the edge of the Trowel Point to iron across the heart on the fast2fuse.

6. Peel up the edge of the heart and remove it from the fast2fuse to reveal a speckled heart image.

Remove foil to reveal heart image.

VARIATION

Die-cut shapes are also great to use as layers and embellishments. Simply hot stamp and apply pigmented mica powder as described. This technique also works great on painted felt.

Die-cut shapes hot stamped with Creative Textile Tool

TYVEK

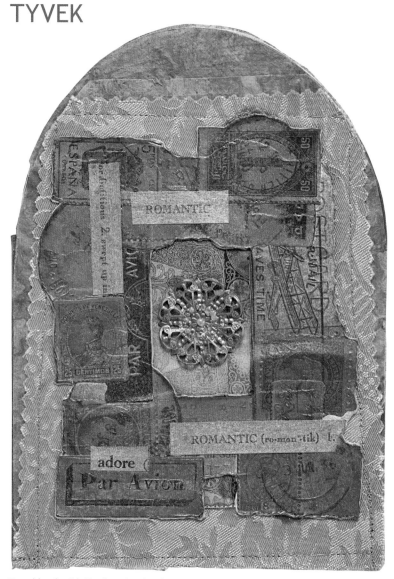

Board book with Tyvek as focal point

I love the results of painting Tyvek with watercolors, fluid acrylics, and alcohol inks. This technique recycles Tyvek envelopes, scrapbook stickers, and papers left over from previous projects. When finished, the result is a very unique, custom-designed, fabriclike material.

MATERIALS

- Tyvek (from new or used envelopes)
- Scrapbook stickers
- Scrapbook paper
- Watercolor spray paints, 2 colors (Radiant Rain Misters by LuminArte)
- Matte medium (by Liquitex)
- Pigment inkpad (Brilliance by Tsukineko)
- Flat paintbrush
- Rubber stamp
- Creative Textile Tool (Walnut Hollow)
- Tempered glass, heat-resistant mat (Walnut Hollow)

HOW TO

1. Spray Tyvek with watercolor paints, alternating between the 2 colors. Let the colors dry between coats.

Spray Tyvek with watercolors.

2. Tear strips of scrapbook papers into irregularly sized pieces. Use a paintbrush to apply a thin layer of matte medium on the Tyvek. While the Tyvek is still wet, randomly apply the paper strips, using more matte medium to cover the strips. Leave open spaces between the papers. Let dry between coats.

3. Randomly apply scrapbook stickers to the painted Tyvek. The stickers should overlap some of the scrapbook papers. Leave some open spaces between the stickers.

Apply stickers to Tyvek.

4. Spray watercolors randomly onto the stickers. Let dry.

Spray watercolors onto stickers.

5. Rubber stamp images onto the Tyvek.

Stamp images onto Tyvek.

6. Use the Creative Textile Tool with the Tapered Point attachment. Working on a glass mat, use the tapered point to randomly cut open areas between the stickers and papers. Do not cut all the areas; leave some open areas between the stickers and papers.

Cut areas between stickers using Tapered Point attachment.

 VARIATION

For added detail, place fabric or papers behind the cut-out areas.

LUTRADUR AND DRYER SHEETS

Postcard with painted and stencil-cut Lutradur. Also shown are Inchie embellishment, embossed paper, and painted muslin.

Lutradur that has been dry brushed with acrylics can be stamped or stenciled and then cut with the Creative Textile Tool. Another option for Lutradur is to print images directly on 8½″ × 11″ sheets run through the paper bed of a home printer. If jamming is an issue, tape the Lutradur to a piece of 8½″ × 11″ freezer paper and print as usual.

Used dryer sheets are also a great material to use in mixed-media art-work. Paint them with acrylic paints and cut them into desired shapes.

MATERIALS
- Lutradur
- Dryer sheets (optional)
- Acrylic fluid paints, 1–2 colors (Golden Fluid Acrylics)
- Pigment inkpad (Brilliance by Tsukineko)
- Watermark inkpad (VersaMark by Tsukineko)
- Pigmented mica powders (Pearl Ex Pigment Powder by Jacquard)
- Water
- Repositionable craft spray (404 Spray and Fix by J. T. Trading)
- Flat paintbrush
- Brass stencil or chipboard embellishments
- Creative Textile Tool with Tapered Point (Walnut Hollow)
- Tempered glass, heat-resistant mat (Walnut Hollow)

HOW TO
1. Paint the Lutradur with fluid acrylic paints diluted with a small amount of water (these paints are very concentrated). Let dry.

2. Spray the back of a brass stencil with repositionable craft spray and place it on the Lutradur.

3. Place the Lutradur on a glass mat. Use the Creative Textile Tool with the Tapered Point attached to cut away the Lutradur through the brass stencil.

Cut through stencil using Creative Textile Tool.

4. Ink the Lutradur with a watermark inkpad.

Apply watermark inkpad onto Lutradur.

5. Use a paintbrush to apply 2 or 3 colors of the pigmented mica powder to the watermark stamp on the Lutradur.

Apply pigmented mica powder to Lutradur.

✻ Chipboard elements, commonly used for scrapbooking, make great templates if you don't have brass stencils.

✻ Acrylic-painted dryer sheets also work wonderfully with this technique. Repeat the same steps for cutting Lutradur.

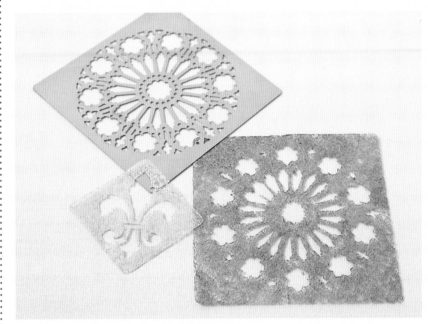

Acrylic-painted dryer sheets cut with stencil.

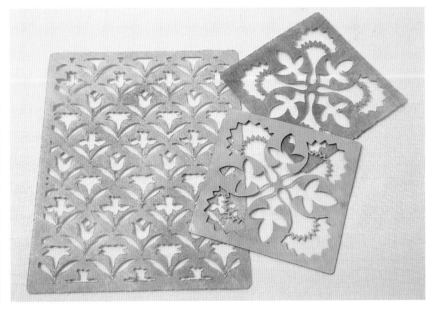

Examples of cut Lutradur

TIP

Lutradur can also be "zapped" with a heat gun for added texture.

distressing

I have always liked the look of vintage fabrics and embellishments such as old lace. Sometimes those beautiful old materials are not available, and new ones need to be purchased instead. The following techniques can be used to age, tone down the color, or change the appearance of supplies such as paper or fabric.

Supplies before being distressed

Supplies after being distressed

DISTRESSING WITH TEA OR COFFEE

Quilt with tea-dyed muslin

Tea dyeing gives a vintage look to fabrics. I often use coffee or tea to tone down the color of my fabrics or to give plain muslin or silk a darker, sepia color. This tea-dyed fabric can then be used as a base for other techniques. **Note:** Tea dyeing works best on natural fibers.

MATERIALS

- Fabric
- Tea bags, regular or herbal
- Brewed coffee (optional)
- Spray bottle (optional)
- Boiling water
- Vanilla extract (optional)

HOW TO

1. Place tea bags in a pot of boiling water. I suggest using 2 or 3 tea bags per 8 ounces of water. Let the tea steep for approximately 5–10 minutes. Remove the tea bags from the water.

2. Soak the fabric in the tea bath for 10–15 minutes. The longer the fabric is kept in the tea, the darker it will become.

3. Remove the fabric from the tea bath and let it dry.

VARIATIONS

* Use hot coffee instead of tea for a darker effect.

* For a lighter tinge, use herbal teas, such as peach or raspberry.

* For a quick effect, place steeped tea into a spray bottle and spray it onto the fabric.

* Add vanilla extract to the tea bath to give fabric a lovely scent.

FABRIC DYE

Canvas with overdyed fabric swatches

Another method I use to distress or age my fabric is to spray it or submerge it in tan fabric dye. Tan Rit Dye is readily available at grocery and craft stores and comes in both liquid and powder form. For the best results, simply follow the manufacturer's instructions.

Left to right: Tan Rit-dyed fabric, plain fabric, orange Rit-dyed fabric

MATERIALS

- Fabric
- Fabric dye (by Rit)
- Diluted Fluid Acrylics (by Golden)

TIP
When dyeing large amounts of muslin or printed fabrics, use the washing machine method listed on the package.

I also like to use other colors of Rit Dye to overdye my fabric. Over-dyeing means dyeing a printed fabric to achieve a darker shade or changing the total color of the fabric without removing the original color.

VARIATION
Use diluted fluid acrylics to overdye fabric. Simply wet the fabric and paint the diluted acrylics directly onto the fabric. Let dry. Start with a ratio of 1 part acrylic to 1 part water. Adjust the ratio according to the desired intensity of the color.

INK

Postcard with ink-distressed Lutradur and muslin

Bottles of dye ink (reinkers) can be mixed with water and applied to paper or fabric to give it a vintage appearance. This type of ink is especially great for dyeing lace because it is fade-resistant, easily applied, and water-based for easy cleanup. Experiment with swatches first to see how much water should be added to the ink before applying it to your project.

MATERIALS
- Paper or fabric
- Lutradur (optional)
- Bottled dye ink (Adirondack Dye Reinkers by Ranger)
- Dye inkpad (Tim Holtz Distress Ink by Ranger; optional)
- Water
- Cosmetic sponge (optional)

TIP
For a fast effect, use a cosmetic sponge and dye inkpad to brush dye ink onto the fabric.

SPRAY PAINT

Spray-painted fabric

A very easy way to add instant age to fabric is to spray it with spray paint. Products such as Design Master's Glossy Wood Tone work nicely.

assembling
the layers

Various layered projects

We are now ready to assemble elements made with various techniques into finished pieces of art. Assembling the layered pieces of a mixed-media creation is a crucial step in achieving a visually interesting finished piece. I suggest creating a book of technique samples or swatches that you can reference when needed.

COMPOSITION

Canvas swatch book of ideas and techniques

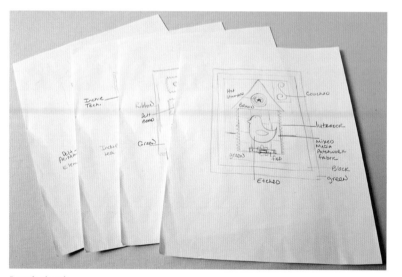

Rough sketch

Start with a sketch or rough drawing of your project. Make notes on where you think elements and colors should be placed. Decide approximately what size you want the finished piece to be.

CREATIVE IDEAS

Keep a journal of ideas or keep paper handy for random ideas that come to mind. These ideas and sketches do not have to be perfect and can definitely be messy. *Only you need to understand them.*

Take a photo of your arrangement as you design. Use this for later reference. Live with your design for a day or two—you may change your mind on a color combination or decide to add or subtract an element.

Buy fabrics you like right away; don't wait or they could be gone next time you want them. Fat quarter bundles of fabrics are convenient and give you a nice variety and assortment of color.

COLOR

I am inspired by color. It is my stepping-off point. We all have our favorite colors that we like to wear or decorate our homes with. The same holds true when creating artwork: We all have colors we are drawn to. Some people use nature as their inspiration. I often see a fabric grouping or paper pattern and am inspired to design with it. I suggest using the 3-in-1 Color Tool, available from C&T Publishing, as a source of good color combinations.

Start a fabric stash and an embellishment stash and organize them by color—this makes it easy to gather all the materials you need (paint, paper, fabric, trims, etc.) for a given project.

TECHNIQUE

Decide what techniques you think will best suit your composition. I often use multiple techniques in one piece of art. As you design your piece, think through which techniques will provide the textures and patterns you need.

BALANCE

Lay out and audition your design elements, arranging them to see whether the artwork looks balanced. Ask yourself the following questions:

◾ Is the arrangement of the elements pleasing to the eye?

◾ Is the color combination appealing?

◾ Is there too much—or not enough—embellishment?

◾ Do any of the elements overpower the others?

◾ Do I want the piece to be symmetrical or asymmetrical? (Symmetry is when both sides of an art piece are equally balanced. If you were to draw a line down the middle of the art piece, the design element would be the same on each side.)

CONSTRUCTION AND FINISHING

1. Once the design elements are in place and you are happy with the composition, put everything in place.

2. Add free-motion embroidery, such as stitch doodling, and decorative stitches.

3. I finish my art quilts with Steam-A-Seam 2 binding: Fuse the Steam-A-Seam 2 onto fabric and cut it into strips. Sandwich the art quilt between these strips and iron them in place. All raw edges of the quilt should be covered by the binding. Traditional quilt binding techniques can also be used.

 TIP

If you are using ephemera or vintage photos in your work, print them onto inkjet canvas sheets or pretreated fabric sheets that are made to run through the printer.

SMALL PROJECT IDEAS

Small projects, such as ATCs, postcards, or what I call snippet squares, are a great way to get started working with mixed media. These small pieces allow you to experiment with various techniques, bases, and embellishments. They can stand alone as small works of art or be incorporated into larger projects as design elements. All of the techniques in this book can be turned into small projects simply by following these general steps.

1. Cut the material made from your chosen technique into the size desired for your project (ATC, below; postcard, page 76; or snippet, page 76).

2. For added support, cut a piece of watercolor paper the same size and adhere it to the back of the artwork.

3. Adorn the project with embellishments, such as beads and buttons and scraps from previous projects.

ARTIST TRADING CARDS (ATCs)

ATC examples

ATCs are little works of art. The rules of ATCs are simple: They must measure 2½″ × 3½″, and they can be made from any medium you wish. ATCs get their name from being traded from one person to another. Any of the techniques in this book will work wonderfully for creating ATCs.

POSTCARDS

Postcard examples

Postcards are both functional and fun to make. The standard sizes of postcards are 3½″ × 5″, 4″ × 6″, 5″ × 5″, and 8″ × 6″. Simply use any of the techniques presented in this book and adhere the finished piece to heavy cardstock or watercolor paper. Then trim to one of the four postcard sizes.

SNIPPETS

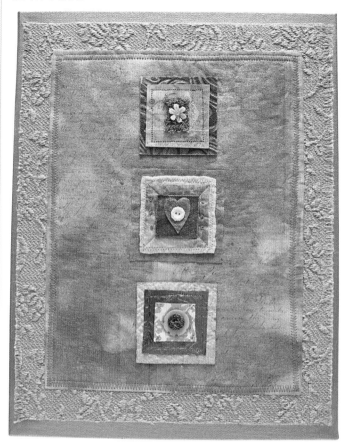

Quilt with snippets

Snippets is the term I use to describe 2″–3″ squares made with leftover bits and pieces from mixed-media creations. Simply cut your materials into 2″–3″ squares and use them as embellishments, pins, and layers. You can also use your leftover pieces of lace, trims, and fibers to decorate the snippets.

canvas quilt

Finished size: 9″ × 12″

I love using canvas as a substrate for my art quilts. I often incorporate the frayed edge of the fabric as a design element. Here, I stamped silk, etched canvas, and embossed craft foam to complete my design.

INSPIRATION

A heart with wings is an iconic image that I use frequently. To me, it represents the idea that doing something you love gives you the wings to accomplish your dreams.

This canvas quilt was the first piece of art that I created for this book. I had made a piece of polished pigment-stamped silk while practicing the technique. That silk piece was my starting point. I loved the color combination of blue, green, and purple tones. I also really liked the raw edge of the silk and decided not to trim it, because it represents my belief that artwork does not have to be perfect in order to be visually appealing.

Having chosen the color palette and heart with wings as my focal point, I decided I wanted this piece to be very dimensional, with many layers built upon a canvas board substrate. I loved combining the different textures of the materials—velvet, felt, silk, cotton fabric, etched canvas, and embossed craft foam each layered upon the other, graduating in size until the embossed heart and wings rested on top.

I collected fabrics, beads, and my design elements/technique materials and auditioned them to see how I wanted them presented on the canvas. When it was all in place, I machine stitched the fabrics to one another and adhered it all to the painted canvas with gel medium.

The round felt beads alone would not be appealing enough, so I added fibers and glass beads. Layering the felt beads on the lace gave them the visual prominence I desired.

My goal with this artwork was to show that fabric art does not always need to be a traditional quilt with a batting layer. Fabric art can also be represented with another medium such as canvas.

MATERIALS

Your own creation will be a unique work of art. You may choose to change the size of the elements or make them from a completely different material. Following are the general *materials I used to make the featured project.*

- ▨ Canvas board
- ▨ Canvas sheet
- ▨ Wool felt
- ▨ Various sizes and colors of coordinating fabric scraps
- ▨ Scraps of silk
- ▨ Scraps of lavender velvet and lace
- ▨ Craft foam
- ▨ Fused Angelina or Crystalina fibers
- ▨ Metallic acrylic paints
- ▨ Alcohol inks
- ▨ Pigmented mica powder (Pearl Ex Pigment Powder by Jacquard)
- ▨ Matte gel medium
- ▨ Sewing thread
- ▨ Metallic embroidery fibers or floss
- ▨ Felt beads
- ▨ Seed beads
- ▨ Metal findings
- ▨ Rubber stamps
- ▨ Paintbrush
- ▨ Embroidery needle
- ▨ Plain and decorative-edge scissors
- ▨ Cosmetic sponges

DESIGN ELEMENTS

For specific directions and materials to make these elements, see the referenced section. Keep in mind that your work is your own creation, and it can include all or none of the elements I have included here. Explore and have fun!

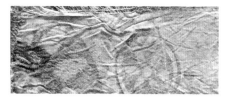

Polished pigment-stamped silk (see Layered Painting and Stamping on Silk, page 29)

Heart shape (see Embossed Angelina and Crystalina, page 60)

Embroidery and beads used as embellishment

Etched canvas sheet (see Etched Canvas, page 62)

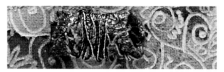

Felt bead, painted and wrapped with metallic fibers (see Felt Beads, page 48)

Embossed craft foam, using hearts and wing stamps (see Embossed Craft Foam, page 59)

birdhouse quilt

Finished size: 12″ × 15″

Easy Mixed-Media Patchwork Fabric (page 34) was the main technique used for this cute little birdhouse quilt. This quilt is a good example of how hot-stamped elements (on roof of birdhouse) and etched canvas (bird) can add interest to your design.

INSPIRATION

Birds are another favorite theme for my artwork. I also love houses and decided to incorporate both into this quilt.

I decided to make the house portion of the quilt with Easy Mixed-Media Patchwork Fabric (page 34). I considered using the Nontraditional Patchwork Fabric (page 38) but decided that the stiffness of the mixed-media fabric would be a stronger design element. I placed cut Lutradur (page 68) under the house as an added design element.

This quilt is an example of how a problem can turn into a design advantage. I wanted to use the green wool, but one of the corners had been cut away. I decided to use it anyway and incorporated the cut-out portion as a design element in the upper-right corner.

I also knew I wanted to use hot techniques on this quilt. I chose to use etching on the canvas bird to give it more texture and interest.

I like how the layered, hot-stamped felt circles give the roof more character. The brown in the circles coordinates well with the brown of the bird and the roof.

I added the metal butterfly, dryer sheet flower, and fast2fuse embellishments to anchor the quilt and add more interest to the overall design of the quilt.

MATERIALS

Your own creation will be a unique work of art. You may choose to change the size of the elements or make them from a completely different material. Following are the general materials I used to make the featured project.

- Scraps of upholstery-weight black brocade and green fabric
- Various sizes and colors of coordinating fabric scraps
- Binding fabric
- Scraps of light and dark wool
- Scraps of brown stripe fabric
- Batting
- Thin metallic embroidery fibers
- Double-sided fusible web (Steam-A-Seam 2)
- Fabric adhesive
- Repositionable craft spray
- Seed beads
- Metal findings
- Sewing machine thread
- Matching button thread
- Embroidery needle
- Small-eyed beading needle
- Disappearing fabric marker
- Decorative-edge fabric scissors
- Metal ruler with zigzag edge
- Pins
- Iron
- Creative Textile Tool (Walnut Hollow)

DESIGN ELEMENTS

For specific directions and materials to make these elements, see the referenced section. Keep in mind that your work is your own creation, and it can include all or none of the elements I have included here. Explore and have fun!

One strip of patchwork fabric, 5½″ × 7″ (see Easy Mixed-Media Patchwork Fabric, page 34)

One bird and wing (see Template Patterns, page 81, Etched Canvas, page 62, and Painting Wool Felt with Polished Pigments, page 19)

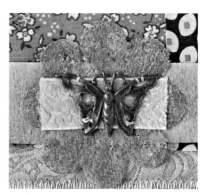

Scalloped, painted dryer sheet (see Lutradur and Dryer Sheets, page 68)

TEMPLATE PATTERNS

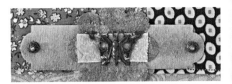

Watercolor-painted fast2fuse embellishment bar (see Painting fast2fuse with Watercolors, page 22)

One etched velvet ribbon, 1½″ × ½″ (see Etched Velvet, page 57)

Three stacked, die-cut, hot-stamped felt circles (see Hot Stamping, page 65)

Two strips gold-painted Lutradur, each 6½″ × 7″, cut with Tapered Point of the Creative Textile Tool and zigzag-design metal ruler (see Lutradur and Dryer Sheets, page 68)

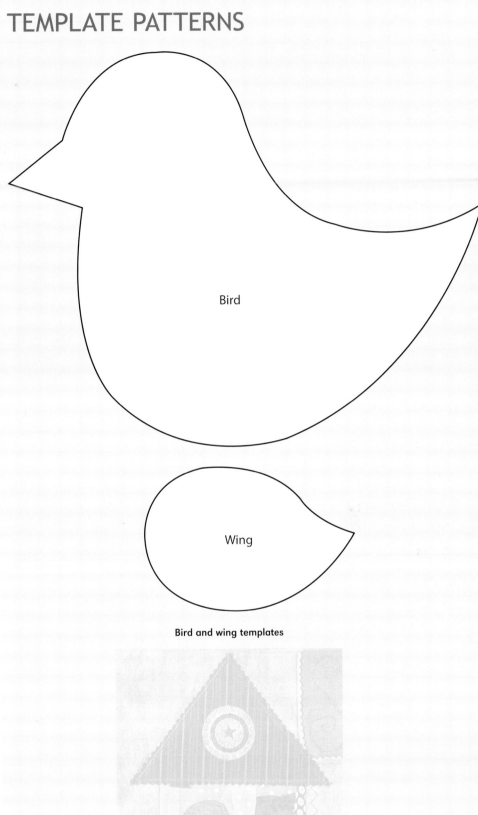

Bird

Wing

Bird and wing templates

black, white,
and red quilt

Finished size: 12½″ × 14½″

One of the main techniques in this quilt is what I call nontraditional patch-work fabric—a patchwork of unequal fabric squares, layered upon each other, with rough, unfinished edges. This technique can use up those small leftover pieces from other fabric projects.

INSPIRATION

This quilt was created with Nontraditional Patchwork Fabric (page 38), which is patchwork but not in the traditional sense. With this technique, the raw edges are celebrated as part of the design.

I normally gravitate toward subtle colors. With this quilt, however, I wanted to wander out of my comfort zone and use more dramatic colors. I had a bunch of red, white, and black fabrics that I wanted to incorporate together in one piece. Layering them and creating the patchwork base were my jumping-off point for this quilt.

My design elements are often placed in the center of the artwork. Again, I decided to stray from my usual thinking and place the photo slightly off center.

I love vintage photographs and frequently print them onto inkjet canvas to use in my work. Using the canvas opened up such design possibilities as etching a border. I used a swirl design, another favorite design element of mine.

I decided that most of the embellishments would be black or gray or, in the case of the altered ribbon, both. That way they would be more pronounced. I arranged and re-arranged them on the quilt until I was comfortable with their placement.

MATERIALS

Your own creation will be a unique work of art. You may choose to change the size of the elements or make them from a completely different material. Following are the general materials I used to make the featured project.

- Diamond print fabric
- Various sizes and colors of coordinating fabric scraps
- Binding fabric
- Two-sided fusible web (Steam-A-Seam 2)
- Batting
- Photo printed onto inkjet canvas
- 2 vintage buttons
- Black embroidery floss
- Sewing machine thread
- Pigmented mica powder (Pearl Ex Pigment Powder by Jacquard)
- Fabric adhesive (Fabri-Tac)

DESIGN ELEMENTS

For specific directions and materials to make these elements, see the referenced section. Keep in mind that your work is your own creation, and it can include all or none of the elements I have included here. Explore and have fun!

One polished pigment-stamped silk square, 3½″ × 3½″ (see **Layered Painting and Stamping on Silk, page 29**)

One piece altered lace, 2½″ × 1¾″ (see **Altered Lace, page 47**)

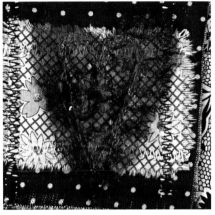

One free-form needle-felted organza heart, 2″ (see **Needle Felting, page 41**)

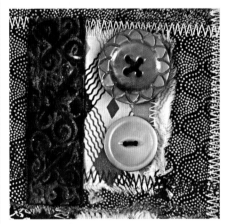

Etched black velvet ribbon, ½″ × 2¼″ and, on facing page, ½″ × 3″ (see **Etched Velvet, page 57**)

1 etched photo, 3¼″ × 5¼″ (see **Etched Canvas, page 62**)

flower sampler quilt

Finished size: 12″ × 12″

I love the soft wispy colors of this quilt. This is a good example of how paper and fabric can be combined to create different textures.

INSPIRATION

The inspiration for this quilt started with the variegated script paper shown under the flower with the stem. I loved its delicate colors and the script on it. I am always drawn to rubber stamps and decorative papers that have script or text on them, and I incorporate them whenever possible.

I decided that this particular color combination would be my palette and jumping-off point. I wanted this quilt to have a vintage, faded, timeworn look. The pale palette reminded me of spring and flowers, so I decided to incorporate as many flowers with different textures (such as fabric, chipboard, and paper) as I could.

I also knew I wanted to make a sampler of many techniques, including both paper and fabric elements, in an uneven patchwork design. When deciding how I wanted to layer certain areas of the quilt, the scripted paper on its own looked blank. I realized that as a paper background, it would give the flower on top more prominence. The fleur-de-lys (in the upper-right corner) is given added importance by placing it on top of painted Lutradur and pink dotted paper.

I wanted to break up areas of the quilt into distinct regions, so I used tea-dyed lace to both separate the elements and blend colorwise.

This artwork hangs in my studio as an inspiration piece and gives me a visual prompt when deciding what techniques to use in future projects.

MATERIALS

Your own creation will be a unique work of art. You may choose to change the size of the elements or make them from a completely different material. Following are the general materials I used to make the featured project.

- Various sizes and colors of coordinating fabric scraps
- Binding fabric
- Batting
- Chipboard
- Matching button thread
- Double-sided fusible web (Steam-A-Seam 2)
- Fabric adhesive (Fabri-Tac)
- Repositionable craft spray
- Disappearing fabric marker
- Decorative-edge fabric scissors
- Iron

DESIGN ELEMENTS

For specific directions and materials to make these elements, see the referenced section. Keep in mind that your work is your own creation, and it can include all or none of the elements I have included here. Explore and have fun!

An additional material—chipboard—is used in this project. Chipboard is a thin cardboard material made from chipped and pressed waste wood and paper products, along with a binder material. It is available precut in a variety of shapes, such as flowers, swirls, and frames. Chipboard, which can be found in the scrapbook department of craft stores, can be painted and/or stamped with either rubber, foam, or hot stamps using the Creative Textile Tool (see page 12). It can also be cut with the hot tool and used as a stencil in stamping or painting another design element. The possibilities are endless!

Tissue fabric block, 3″ × 3″ (see Tissue Fabric, page 33) behind painted chipboard flower made with a technique similar to Dry Brushing with Paint, page 18

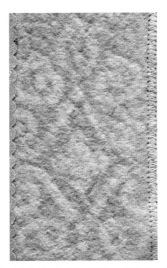

Bleached felt block, 3″ × 5″ (see Painting Felt with Bleach, page 21)

Paintstik-embellished muslin block, 3″ × 4″ (see Shiva Paintstiks on Muslin, page 24)

Needle-felted fabric block, 5″ × 5″ (see Needle Felting, page 41)

Written script paper behind flower with pearl-bead and acrylic-painted center and tea-dyed velvet leaves, 5″ × 7″

Dotted paper, 4″ × 5″

One piece altered ribbon, 1½″ × 4″
(see Altered Ribbon, page 47)

Crayon on muslin block, 4″ × 4″ (see Melted
Crayon on Muslin, page 25) with fabric
flowers (see Distressing with Tea or Coffee,
page 71)

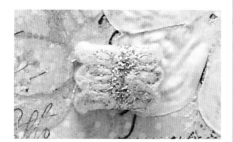

Felt bead, ¾″ (see Felt Beads, page 48)

Painted fleur-de-lys cut from Lutradur
mounted on painted Lutradur (see Lutradur
and Dryer Sheets, page 68)

Etched green velvet ribbon, 8″ × ½″
(see Etched Velvet, page 57)

Pearl bead, 6mm diameter

Silver acrylic-painted metal flower
(see Dry Brushing with Paint using
metallic acrylic paint, page 18)

One tea-dyed fabric flower (see Distressing
with Tea or Coffee, page 71)

Two tea-dyed velvet leaves (see Distressing
with Tea or Coffee, page 71)

One piece tea-dyed lace, ½″ × 3″ (see
Distressing with Tea or Coffee, page 71)

paper quilt

Finished size: 12″ × 12″

This quilt—a combination of both paper and fabric—is one of my favorites. I love finding papers and fabrics that coordinate and then making my own material to go with them. In this case, my creation was tissue fabric. This quilt has a free-form binding of overlapping paper and fabrics.

INSPIRATION

The inspiration for this artwork came from the tissue fabric base. I love the look of monochromatic colors and wispy shades of white layered on top of each other. I had saved some pretty tissue paper that came with a gift. I really loved the paper's blue floral design and thought a white-washed look would be interesting.

I collect vintage button cards. This particular one complemented the tissue fabric background nicely, so I made the button card the focal point of the quilt.

I had the idea that a binding incorporating both paper and fabric would give this piece more interest, so I machine stitched the binding fabrics and papers overlapping each other. When the first layered binding was applied, however, it still looked uninteresting, so I added another layer of binding in some (but not all) areas to create extra detail and interest.

Because I wanted the quilt to be serene and peaceful, I used tea dyeing and other distressing techniques to age the leaves and Tyvek tag, which tied it all together visually with the whitewashed tissue fabric.

MATERIALS

Your own creation will be a unique work of art. You may choose to change the size of the elements or make them from a completely different material. Following are the general materials I used to make the featured project.

- 140-weight watercolor paper
- Coordinating handmade papers
- Various sizes and colors of coordinating fabric scraps
- Batting
- 1 vintage button card
- Matching button thread
- 1 snippet of lace
- 2 small silk leaves
- 1 small button
- Scrap of tulle
- 1 small piece cream ribbon
- Double-sided fusible web (Steam-A-Seam 2)
- Repositionable craft spray
- Paper adhesive
- Paper hole punch
- Decorative-edge scissors
- Iron

DESIGN ELEMENTS

For specific directions and materials to make these elements, see the referenced section. Keep in mind that your work is your own creation, and it can include all or none of the elements I have included here. Explore and have fun!

Square of tissue fabric, 12″ × 12″ (see Tissue Fabric, page 33)

Tea-dyed batting

Tea-dyed batting, 5½″ × 6¾″ (see Distressing with Tea or Coffee, page 71)

Painted and stamped Lutradur pocket, 6½″ × 6½″ (see Lutradur and Dryer Sheets, page 68)

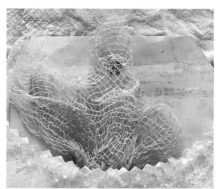

Tea-dyed Tyvek tag with ink distress and tea-dyed cheesecloth, 6½″ × 6½″ (see Distressing with Tea or Coffee, page 71, and Ink, page 72)

Needle-felted organza heart, 1″–2″ (see Needle Felting, page 41), and silk leaves with ink distress

gallery

Size: 8½″ × 8½″

▨ fast2fuse book painted with Dye-Na-Flow and stenciled with metallic acrylic paint; edges hot stamped with Creative Textile Tool

▨ **Elements:** embellished with "plus-size" Inchies, felt beads, and hot-stamped elements

▨ *Note: This book would make a great technique swatch book.*

Size: 8″ × 8″

▨ Board book base covered with "Waste not, want not" freezer paper

▨ **Elements:** bleached felt; Stitch-N-Tear; altered lace; couched threads

Finished size: 12″ × 14″

▨ Quilt with layered, stamped muslin base

▨ **Elements:** crayon melted on muslin; stencil-cut Lutradur; painted, die-cut, and hot-stamped fast2fuse frame; free-motion embroidery; snippet squares; cut Lutradur and dryer sheets; hot-stamped, painted felt; free-form scrap fabric; easy mixed-media patchwork fabric; etched canvas

Finished size: 22″ × 11″

▨ Designs mounted on 8″ × 6″ canvas boards; canvas boards mounted on stiffened bleached felt and then onto Dye-Na-Flow-painted fast2fuse

▨ Elements: craft foam bead; painted and stamped Lutradur; needle-felted organza; embossed craft foam; painted dryer sheet; felt painted with polished pigments; altered ribbon

Finished size: 11″ × 14½″

▨ Quilt on base of Dye-Na-Flow-painted fast2fuse, with focal point of free-form scrap fabric

▨ Elements: silk carrier rod waste; "plus-size" Inchies; embroidered felt flower mounted on striped upholstery fabric

Finished size: 12½″ × 16½″

▨ Quilt on base of nontraditional patchwork fabric; focal point is a 5″ × 6½″ square made with "plus-size" Inchies technique with edges hot-stamped with the Creative Textile Tool

▨ Elements: all technique materials made into ATCs, then stitched onto quilt; free-motion stitched design elements added for texture and visual interest

Finished size: 13″ × 15″

■ Quilt mounted on base of Dye-Na-Flow-painted fast2fuse with fused Angelina fibers

■ Elements: bleached felt; embossed batting; watercolor-painted fast2fuse; buttons; etched velvet; hot-stamped felt; machine-stitched embellishment strip; silk fusion

Finished size: 12½″ × 14½″

■ Quilt with altered ribbon and lace background

■ Elements: easy mixed-media patchwork fabric for dress

■ House board book covered with tissue fabric

■ Elements: window embellished with painted, embossed felt and silk fusion

Finished size: 11″ × 13″

■ Purchased frame covered with base of uncut Inchies technique on fast2fuse

■ **Elements:** Inchies

Size: 9″ × 12″

■ **Canvas board fabric collage painted with fluid acrylics**

■ **Elements:** free-form scrap fabric; painted fast2fuse frame; etched velvet painted with stencil; painted batting; embossed craft foam; embossed batting; silk fusion

Finished size: 10″ × 14″

■ Base of bleached felt stiffened with textile medium for added support

■ **Elements:** embossed craft foam; felt painted with polished pigments; snippet square with painted fast2fuse; Ultra Thick Embossing Enamel embellishment on easy mixed-media patchwork fabric; painted, embossed felt; hot-stamped felt

Size: 3″ × 3″

■ **Board book covered with tissue fabric**

■ **Elements:** Tissue fabric, distressed fabric flower

Size: 6″ × 12″

■ Layered display board book

■ **Elements:** nontraditional patchwork fabric base with cheesecloth and etched photo

Finished size: 9½″ × 11″

■ **Quilt with base of uncut Inchies on fast2fuse**

■ **Elements:** Inchies and "plus-size" Inchies for embellishment; free-motion embroidery

■ **Box covered with scripted paper and free-form scrap fabric trim**

■ **Elements:** Solvron heart created with black velvet

Finished size: 14″ × 16″

■ **Quilt on base of free-form fabric scraps stitched onto a felt base**

■ **Elements:** printed and punched Stitch-N-Tear; embossing powders on batting; painted thread fabric; painted Lutradur cut using chipboard stencil and distressed with a heat gun; silk fusion; oil paintsticks on silk; painted and stamped muslin; painted batting; felt painted with polished pigments; Tyvek

resources

3M
Scotchgard Fabric Protector
www.3M.com
800-713-6329

Artgirlz
Felt beads, pewter metal findings
www.artgirlz.com
866-507-4822

Beacon Adhesives
Zip Dry Paper Adhesive, Fabri-Tac
Fabric Adhesive, Stiffen Stuff
www.beacon1.com
914-699-3405

Bear Thread Designs, Inc.
Grip-n-Grip nonslip sheet
www.BearThreadDesigns.com
281-462-0661

Bo-Nash North America
Bonding Agent 007
www.bonash.com
800-527-8811

C&T Publishing
Board books, fast2fuse, Quilter's
Freezer Paper Sheets, Quilter's Vinyl,
and 3-in-1 Color Tool
www.ctpub.com
800-284-1114

Clover Needlecraft, Inc.
Needle Felting Tool and Brush Mat,
Handheld Felting Needles
www.clover-usa.com
800-233-1703

Crayola
Crayons
www.crayola.com
610-253-6271

DecoArt, Inc.
Fabric Painting Medium, Liquid Varnish
www.decoart.com
800-367-3047

Design Master Color Tool, Inc.
Glossy Wood Tone
www.dmcolor.com
303-443-5214

Deval Products LLC
Simply Spray
www.simplyspray.com
800-261-4772

Dream Weaver Brass Stencils
Brass stencils
www.dreamweaverstencils.com
909-824-8343

Dritz Quilting/Omnigrid/Prym
Consumer USA, Inc.
Omnigrip rulers, rotary cutters, markers,
mats and scissors
www.omnigrid.com

DuPont
Tyvek
www.dupont.com/Tyvek/en_US/
800-448-9835

Fairfield Processing
Nature-fil Bamboo Batting
www.poly-fil.com
800-980-8000

Fredrix Art Canvas, Tara Materials, Inc.
Canvas Boards, Canvas Sheets, and
Creative Edge Canvas
www.fredrixartistcanvas.com
800-241-8129

Golden Artist Colors, Inc
Fluid Acrylics
www.goldenpaints.com
800-959-6543

Gutermann
Thread
www.gutermann.com
888-488-3762

J. T. Trading Corporation
Fabric Shield, 404 Spray and Fix
www.sprayandfix.com
860-350-5565

Janome
Sewing machines
www.janome.com

Krylon Products Group
Workable Fixatif, Leafing Pens, Spray
Varnish
www.krylon.com
800-4KRYLON

Laura Murray
Foil and adhesive
www.lauramurraydesigns.com
612-825-1209

Liquitex Artist Materials
Matte Medium, Matte Gel Medium
www.liquitex.com
888-422-7954

LuminArte, Inc.
Radiant Rain Misters, Pure Color
Concentrate Daubers, Twinkling H20s,
Primary Elements Polished Pigments,
Simple Solutions #1
www.luminarteinc.com
866-229-1544

Loew-Cornell, Inc.
Quality paintbrushes, palette paper
www.loewcornell.com
866-227-9206

Making Memories
Foam stamps
www.makingmemories.com
801-294-0430

McGill, Inc.
Paper punches
wwmcgillinc.com
800-982-9884

Meadowbrook Inventions
Angelina and Crystalina fibers
www.meadowbrookinventions.com
908-766-0606

Nunn Design
Metal embellishment findings
www.nunndesign.com
800-761-3557

Pellon Consumer Products
Stitch-N-Tear, Lutradur
www.shoppellon.com
877-817-0944

Quilter's Resource, Brewer Quilting
and Sewing Supplies
Solvron
www.quiltersresource.com
800-676-6543

Ranger Industries
Tim Holtz Distress Dye Ink and Reinkers,
Adirondack Acrylic Dabbers, Adirondack
Dimensional Pearls, Inkssentials Glossy
Accents, Adirondack Alcohol Inks
www.rangerink.com
732-389-3535

Phoenix Brands LLC
Rit Dye
www.ritdye.com
866-794-0800

Plaid Enterprises, Inc.
Brass stencils
www.plaidonline.com
800-842-4197

Rupert, Gibbon & Spider, Inc.
Lumiere Acrylic Paint, Textile Color,
Dye-Na-Flow, Pearl Ex Pigment Powder,
Colorless Extender, ExtravOrganza,
Inkjet Silk Habotai
www.jacquardproducts.com
800-442-0455

Sizzix
Die-cutting machine
www.sizzix.com
877-355-4766

Sulky
Water-soluble stabilizers
www.sulky.com
800-874-4115

The Warm Company
Steam-A-Seam 2
www.warmcompany.com
425-248-2424

Tsukineko
Brilliance Pigment Ink, StazOn Solvent
Ink, VersaMark Watermark Ink
www.tsukineko.com
425-883-7733

The Vintage Workshop, A Division of
Indygo Junction, Inc.
Click-n-Craft artwork images on CD,
online downloadable images, printable
fabric sheets
www.thevintageworkshop.com
877-546-3946

Vintaj Natural Brass Co.
Natural brass jewelry findings
www.vintaj.com

Walnut Hollow Farms
Creative Textile Tool, glass mat,
wood boxes
www.walnuthollow.com
800-950-5101

Wright's
Lace, trims, and ribbon
www.wrights.com
800-660-0415

YLI Corporation
Thread, embellishment yarn, fibers,
silk carrier rod waste, Painters Mailing
and Trading Cards by Tentakulum
Manufaktur, silk hankies, Painters
Potpourri Packs
www.ylicorp.com
803-985-3100

FABRIC SOURCES

Cotton Patch Mail Order
Fabrics, quilt supplies
www.quiltusa.com
925-283-7883

Dharma Trading Company
Silk, craft supplies, fabric
www.dharmatrading.com
800-542-5227

Fat Quarter Shop
Fat quarters
www.fatquartershop.com
866-826-2069

Hancock's of Paducah
www.hancocks-paducah.com
800-845-8723

Keepsake Quilting
www.keepsakequilting.com
800-525-8086

Mirah's Crafts
Batik fabrics
www.princessmirah.com

Moda Fabrics
Many of the fabrics used for projects
are Moda Designs
www.unitednotions.com
800-527-9447

National Nonwovens
Wool Felt
www.nationalnonwovens.com
800-333-3469

ONLINE CRAFT STORES

Dick Blick
Shiva Paintstiks, Fluid Acrylics, Crayola
Metallic FX Crayons
www.dickblick.com
800-828-4548

Joggles
Textiles, mixed-media supplies,
silk hankies
www.joggles.com
401-615-7696

Quilting Arts
Ink, paint, fibers, Lutradur, Angelina
www.quiltingarts.com
866-698-6989

about the author

Photo by Amy N. Sanavongxay

Rebekah Meier is a self-taught mixed-media
artist and designer. Over the course of more
than 20 years in the craft industry, she has
had her designs appear in such publications as *Altered Couture*, *Better Homes
and Gardens Special Interest Publications*,
Crafts 'n Things, *Create and Decorate*, and
Stampington's Sew Somerset.

Rebekah has authored several other books
on the subjects of weddings, scrapbooking,
and paper crafts. She resides in northern
Illinois with her husband and two sons.

Great Titles

from C&T PUBLISHING

Art Quilt Workbook
JANE DAVILA & ELIN WATERSTON
BONUS GUIDE
EXHIBIT YOUR QUILT
EXERCISES & TECHNIQUES TO IGNITE YOUR CREATIVITY

The Quilter's Directory of EMBELLISHMENTS
46 step-by-step decorative techniques, from appliqué and embroidery to tassels and trims

create your own hand-printed cloth
RAYNA GILLMAN
STAMP, SCREEN & STENCIL WITH EVERYDAY OBJECTS

fabric leftovers
D'Arcy-Jean Milne
Simple, adaptable ways to use up scraps

Creative Art Concepts for papercrafts
An Effortless Approach to Fine Art Techniques
Lea Cioci

Make Spectacular Books
Fabulous Fabric, Skewer & Folded Books